T·E·X·A·S
TREES

T·E·X·A·S
TREES
A Friendly Guide

Paul W. Cox and
Patty Leslie

•

Illustrations by Gloria Merlo
and Sara Harrison

CORONA PUBLISHING COMPANY
San Antonio

Fourth Printing June 1993

Library of Congress Cataloging-in-Publication Data

Cox, Paul W., 1952–
    Texas trees.

    Bibliography: p.
    Includes index.
    1. Trees--Texas. 2. Trees--Texas--Identification.
I. Leslie, Patty, 1957-   . II. Title.
QK188.C69 1988   582.1609764   87-72604
ISBN 0-931722-67-5 (pbk.)
ISBN 0-931722-66-7 (lib. bdg.)

Printed and bound in the United States of America.

FOREWORD

Most countries are known by a single tree. There are the Shillelagh Oaks of Ireland, the original green blanketing of the Emerald Isles; there are the yews of England, source of the longbows that defeated the flower of French chivalry; there is Germany's Black Forest of spruce and fir; there are the ancient olives of Greece and Palestine. Texas, on the other hand, (and despite the fame of the pecan as her state tree) cannot be characterized by a single species. It is too vast a place, both on the map and in the mind.

What's more, due to its lengthy status as a frontier and the simple fact that there are still some fairly extensive forests intact, Texas has developed an extensive body of historical associations. There are hundreds of "historic" trees which just happened to be providing shade in the right spot at the right time. Of course, there are "hanging trees" in abundance, each with its gruesome tale of just or unjust death. In downtown San Antonio, the tall "Sniper's Cypress" still stands, from which a Mexican soldier shot Ben Milam on December 7, 1835. Down on the Rio Grande is an ancient Ebony which serves as the Texas-side anchor for the last hand-pulled ferry on the border. Sam Houston had a knack for picking oak trees for his better moments. There is the Headquarters Oak just north of Gonzales which was Houston's base camp just prior to the battle at San Jacinto. In San Marcos, there is Houston's Kissing Oak, where the gubernatorial candidate kissed a bevy of Texas beauties in 1857.

Texas is one of the few places in the world where war has been declared against a single species of tree. For well over a century, the mesquite waged a uniquely successful campaign against the natural agrarian economy of the human residents. The slash-and-burn mentality engendered by this generations-long ecological combat is with us still — much to the detriment of many other forms of flora and fauna.

Although we have lost virtually all knowledge of the lore and legends attached to native Texas trees by the state's Native American inhabitants, yet there are some trees of near-mythic significance. In the heart of San Antonio, just north of the headwaters of the river, stands a motte of three oaks held sacred by the Ponca tribe. Indians were observed performing rituals on this spot as late as 1924, a practice they described as dating from the "grandfathers of their grandfathers." These holy oaks stand on ground consecrated by — as the archaeologists put it — "12,000 years of continuous human habitation."

Trees and humans have always had a special relationship. The ancient Norse believed that the world axis was the great Ash tree, Yggdrasil. With its roots in hell and its leaves providing fodder for the war steeds of the gods, this tree was where Odin, Christ-like, hung for nine days for the sake of bringing wisdom to mortal men. The God of the Old Testament was pretty particular about His trees and their uses. Noah's ark, for example, was to be made of nothing but gopher wood; the ark of the covenant was to be constructed of Chittamwood. When it came to building the actual temple, only the Cedars of Lebanon would do.

But in the end, it is individual people interacting with individual trees that make the best magic. I spent many afternoons reading in the top of a pecan tree in Dallas when I was in grade school. I still remember the easiest route among the branches, and I still get the desire to climb that tree whenever I drive past it. And annoying as reading in tree shade is in reality, my best memories of favorite books always seem to include leafy green canopies and sun-dappled pages. It is probably impossible to tell tree folk from other people, but I like to think that the person who has a tree in his or her past is simply a better human.

Just because our twentieth-century reality is supported more by steel than by timber, this is no reason to ignore what appears to be a permanent relationship between humankind and trees. Perhaps the average denizen of the urban jungle has truly no need to be able to tell an oak from a pecan. Does a child's ignorance of such things matter? I think so. I recently took a group of children to visit a large hollow cypress tree growing beside the San Antonio River just blocks from downtown. They had no idea that a tree *could* be hollow, much less that a dryad might be imprisoned there. How can the idea of a hollow tree be foreign to us? How can the sacredness of the forest be foreign to us? We do not have to dance beneath the moon in a forest glade to become sensitive to the fact that cutting down the Amazonian rain forests or letting the Black Forest wither beneath acid rain are acts of global suicide. And the first step toward preventing such disasters is to gain some knowledge about the trees around us — those in our yards and parks and nature preserves — some knowledge that goes beyond mere identification.

This is why I rejoice at the publication of this guidebook to the trees of Texas. What makes this book different from other identification guides is its effort to bring people and trees together in a meaningful way, both in the illustrations and in the text. One can still look up, say, a Cedar Elm, and find that it is primarily a Texas tree which grows best in limestone hills and flowers in late summer; but there is more: bits of history, common uses, a bit of the tree lore which has developed in Texas over the last couple of centuries. Whether it is the Texas Hill Country, the Big Thicket, or the *galerias* of South Texas, wherever man and tree have come together there is a rich vein of human interest to be mined.

You can start here.

Bryce Milligan
...author of Daysleepers & Other Poems

ACKNOWLEDGEMENTS

To acknowledge the help of all who assisted us either by technical advice or through needed moral support is not practical here. Unlike the story of the Little Red Hen, we have been helped by many, none of whom have asked for recognition, but a few of whom deserve special mention here.

Scott Ogden, of Aldridge Nursery, provided much in the way of technical advice, as did Mark Peterson with the Texas Forest Service. We are also grateful to Dr. Marshall C. Johnston, University of Texas Botany Department, for reviewing the text and assisting with nomenclature updates. Don Pylant, Horticulturist II at the San Antonio Botanical Center, gave invaluable computer assistance, alleviating a lot of frustration. Three professional associates who helped with much encouragement and positive urgings are Ron Darner, Director of the San Antonio Parks and Recreation Department, Tom Keeter, Services Administrator in the same Department, and last but not least our good friend Eric Tschanz, Director of the San Antonio Botanical Gardens, who never lost faith in our attempt and was a constant source of advice and understanding.

The man who planted the original seed of the book and has nourished its growth at every stage is David Bowen of Corona Publishing Company. Thanks also to Alice Evett for her thorough editing and helpful suggestions. And of course, our families, like any proud parents, should not be overlooked for their constant support and beaming affection for this project.

It is our hope that this will not only be an educational book but will serve to entertain as well.

CONTENTS

Vegetational Areas of Texas

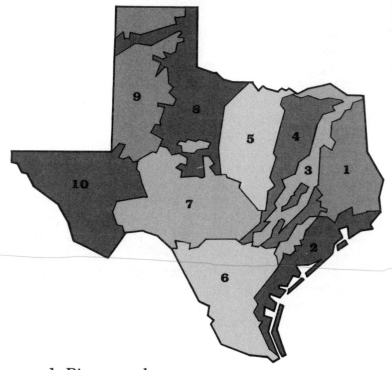

1. Pineywoods
2. Gulf Prairies and Marshes
3. Post Oak Savannah
4. Blackland Prairies
5. Cross Timbers and Prairies
6. South Texas Plains
7. Edwards Plateau
8. Rolling Plains
9. High Plains
10. Trans-Pecos, Mountains and Basins

Adapted from *Texas Plants — A Checklist and Ecological Summary*,
by Frank W. Gould (1962; 1969), Texas Agricultural Experiment Station,
Texas A&M University.

INTRODUCTION

There has always been a certain amount of controversy surrounding the technical definition of a tree. Most people tend to favor: "a single stem to ten feet tall with a six-inch diameter." This would include large shrubby species such as Mexican Buckeye (*Ungnadia speciosa*) and exclude young tree seedlings. Perhaps a more practical definition is the proverb, "If you can walk under it, it's a tree; if you have to walk around it, it's a shrub."

There is so much diversity in Texas vegetation it can be overwhelming. In fact, Texas ranks second only to Florida as having the most native and naturalized exotic species within its boundaries. One good example of plant diversity here is the oaks. Of the approximately 64 North American oak species, 44 are native somewhere in Texas.

Viewed in its entirety, the state can be seen as the place where several great floras converge. The East Texas Piney Woods is the southwestern part of the vast eastern deciduous forests. South Texas represents the northmost reach of the Tamaulipan flora from Mexico.

On the western front, the Trans-Pecos area is mostly Chihuahuan Desert with some Rocky Mountain components at the higher elevations. The Great Plains cover much of North Texas and peter out in the East Central area. In the middle of all this is the Edwards Plateau or "Hill Country," with representatives from the other areas in addition to a number of endemic species. Within the state boundaries these areas combine to form a veritable forest of tree species.

In an effort to help the novice distinguish the trees from the forest, this book has avoided using many technical terms, and we provide a glossary for such necessary terms as might need explanation. The text is arranged according to practical field characteristics, and the Pictorial Leaf Key at the beginning is actually an organized listing of groups based on leaf arrangement and complexity.

The title of "champion" tree is often a fleeting distinction but has been included where the specimen may be open to public access or if it is nationally noteworthy. The status is based on a point system using the sum of the height, average crown spread, and trunk circumference. (To get a rough idea of the trunk diameter, divide the circumference by three.) These individuals represent the extremes a species might reach. The dimensions given at the beginning of each entry are the average sizes usually encountered for a particular tree species.

Each major native entry has an accompanying range map indicating its general area of distribution. Naturalized exotic tree species do not have range maps because they have no naturally occurring area and may be planted throughout the state.

The system for naming plants is somewhat confusing to the uninitiated — and often frustrating to the professional. Most trees have a common name that has been handed down through generations. A few native trees have carried their ancient Indian names into modern nomenclature. Catalpa, Hickory, and Anaqua have all retained at least a corruption of their old Indian titles. The disadvantage of a common name is that often the same one is used in referring to several widely different species. There are species of trees in almost every region of Texas that are locally known as "Ironwood" because they have hard wood. Early settlers, hard pressed to name some trees, would use such elusive terms as "Chittamwood," a reference to a Biblical plant of no relation, or colorful descriptive names like "Grancy Gray Beard."

On the other hand, all plants are appointed scientific names that generally describe some aspect of the plant, honor some individual, event, or location, or carry on a classical name. The scientific name consists of the first — or genus — name plus the specific epithet — or species — title. Groups of similar species are placed in a genus, and a collection of related genera belong to a family. These families are often known and referred to as a result of a particularly well-known genus in that group, e.g., the Rose family, Walnut family, or Olive family. Scientific names provide the ultimate in current nomenclature for referring to a single plant. These names, however, are in a state of constant change as the old literature is continually reviewed, often resulting in several synonymous scientific names for the same plant.

The good thing that can be said for common names is that they rarely change over the years. A Crab Apple, for instance, will always be a Crab Apple, even if the scientific community calls it a *Pyrus ioensis* one day and a *Malus ioensis* the next. Scientific nomenclature in this book for the most part follows that comprehensive work *The Manual of the Vascular Plants of Texas* by Correll and Johnston (1970).

Most trees tend to favor certain soil types or forest

situations. When a set of species occur as a fairly distinct group they can be said to characterize a site and form an association of species known as a "forest" or "cover type." Post Oak, Blackjack Oak, and Texas Hickory, for instance, form a widespread association found on dry hills over much of the eastern half of Texas.

There is a particular succession of plant species that tend to populate different areas. When a major disturbance such as a clear cut, fire, or severe windstorm removes the existing canopy, or if a new sand bar is formed or a cultivated field abandoned, there are fairly distinct associations of species that invade and colonize these new territories. These are usually referred to as "pioneer" species. They are often fast growing, sun loving, and intolerant of shade or competition from other species. The Cottonwood-Willow combination is a typical pioneer community of disturbed areas near water. As these species mature and pass on, they are usually replaced by more tolerant individuals. When the majority of trees are only those that can live and reproduce within their own shade and competitive environment, the forest has reached a "climax" state.

Probably the most common climax cover type in Texas is the Oak-Hickory forest roughly covering the eastern third of the state. In some instances of repeated disturbances such as frequent fires, a successional sequence is kept from reaching its natural trend, resulting in what is termed a "fire subclimax."

Trees are, for the most part, very distinctive members of the plant kingdom. To be able to identify individuals in a forest is an exhilarating experience. With the aid of this field guide, it is hoped the user will learn to know the trees of Texas and will also get a glimpse into the past and see how these prominent members of the plant world influenced the lives of those who depended upon the land for survival.

PICTORIAL LEAF KEY

Grouped according to leaf type and arrangement

I. Needle or scalelike leaves,
   without true flowers, seeds
   borne in a woody or fleshy cone
      A. Bald Cypress, Montezuma
         Cypress (*Taxodium*) pp. 3-5

      B. Pines (*Pines*)   pp. 6-20

      C. Douglas Fir (*Pseudotsuga*)
                      pp. 21-23

      D. Arizona Cypress
         (*Cupressaceae*)   pp. 24-25

      E. Juniper or "cedar"
         (*Juniperus*)   pp. 26-35

II. Scalelike leaves, evergreen with
   pink flowers, fruit a small capsule
   Salt Cedar (*Tamarix*)   pp. 36-37

III. Large fan-shaped leaves
   Palms (*Sabal, Washingtonia*)
                    pp. 38-43

IV. Long leaves, flat or concave,
   sharp-pointed, tough or flexible
   Yuccas (*Yucca*)   pp. 44-52

V. ALTERNATE LEAVES
A. SIMPLE

1. Ginkgo
   (*Ginkgo*)
   pp. 53-55

2. Willows
   (*Salix*)
   pp. 56-58

3. Cottonwoods
   (*Populus*)
   pp. 59-64

4. Hornbeams
   (*Carpinus, Ostrya*)
   pp. 65-66

5. River birch, Alder
   (*Betula, Alnus*)
   pp. 70-73

6. Beech, Chinquapin
   (*Fagus, Castanea*)
   pp. 74-77

7. Oaks (*Quercus*)
   Red Oaks
   White Oaks
   Live Oaks
   pp. 78-130

8. Elms
   (*Ulmus, Planera*)
   pp. 131-142

9. Hackberry
   (*Celtis*)
   pp. 143-146

10. Osage Orange
    (*Maclura*)
    pp. 147-149

11. Mulberry
    (*Morus*)
    pp. 150-152

12. Magnolia
    (*Magnolia*)
    pp. 153-158

13. Paw Paw
    (*Asimina*)
    pp. 159-160

14. Red Bay, Sassafras
    (*Persea, Sassafras*)
    pp. 161-165

15. Witch Hazel
    (*Hamamelis*)
    pp. 166-167

16. Sweetgum
    (*Liquidambar*)
    pp. 168-170

17. Sycamore
    (*Platanus*)
    pp. 171-173

18. Mt. Mahogany
    (*Cercocarpus*)
    pp. 174-175

19. Hawthorns
    (*Crataegus*)
    pp. 176-179

20. Plums, Cherries
    (*Prunus*)
    pp. 180-187

21. Crab Apples
    (*Pyrus*)
    pp. 188-189

22. Loquat
    (*Eriobotrya*)
    pp. 190-191

23. Chinese Tallow
    (*Sapium*)
    pp. 192-193

24. TiTi
    (*Cyrilla*)
    pp. 194-195

25. Holly, Yaupon
    (*Ilex*)
    pp. 196-200

26. Bluewood Condalia
    (*Condalia*)
    pp. 201-202

27. Carolina Buckthorn
    (*Rhamnus*)
    pp. 203-204

28. Basswood
    (*Tilia*)
    pp. 205-207

29. Black Tupelo
    (*Nyssa*)
    pp. 208-210

30. Madrone
    (*Arbutus*)
    pp. 211-213

31. Gum Bumelia
    (*Bumelia*)
    pp. 214-216

32. Snowdrop Tree
    (*Halesia, Styrax*)
    pp. 217-219

xxiii

B. PALMATELY COMPOUND

1. Buckeye
   (*Aesculus*)
   pp. 324-326

2. Chaste Tree
   (*Vitex*)
   pp. 343-344

C. PINNATELY COMPOUND

1. Box Elder
   (*Acer*)
   pp. 322-323

2. Ash
   (*Fraxinus*)
   pp. 333-342

3 Elderberry
   (*Sambucus*)
   pp. 350-352

T · E · X · A · S
TREES

BALD CYPRESS

Taxodium distichum.
Southern Cypress.
Tall deciduous tree over 100 feet tall and 6 feet in diameter. The shape of the crown can be extremely variable but is usually narrowly conical when young, becoming somewhat flattened with slightly drooping branches when mature. The trunk is typically flared at the base ending in long horizontal roots giving it a buttressed appearance.

Leaves — Alternate, feather-like, ½ to ¾ inch in length, pointed at the tip, light green or yellowish green turning rusty brown or red in the fall.

3

Taxodiaceae - Bald Cypress Family

Flowers — Five-inch-long drooping clusters of small male cones with a few female cones at the branch tips, borne in spring.

Fruit — Wrinkled, rounded cones about 1 inch in diameter maturing in the fall.

Twigs — The small lateral twigs drop away with the leaves in the fall. The remaining twigs are thin and smooth with small rounded pale brown buds.

Bark — Gray or light reddish brown, fibrous, with shallow furrows and broad flat ridges.

Bald Cypress could be considered an aquatic tree as it is always found naturally growing in or near surface water. In East Texas it is found in swamps and along rivers, and in Central Texas the tree lines almost every river and major stream bank. On frequently flooded or swampy sites the roots will send up woody conical growths several feet tall called "knees." Although it has not been proven, some believe the purpose of these projections is to bring air to the roots or to serve as anchors in mucky soils. Knees are rarely present on Central Texas trees. Bald Cypress wood is one of the most variable in the United States in regard to color, weight, and durability. Most common is a yellowish sapwood and a brown heartwood, both with distinct growth rings. Because of its resistance to decay, it is used extensively for exterior siding, shingles, dock and bridge timbers, railroad ties, greenhouse benching, and vats.

This is a good ornamental tree because of its fast growth rate, feathery foliage, nice form, and reliable fall color. The tree will grow on a variety of sites but does best near a low area with plenty of water. Fluctuating the water table drastically, whether by man or nature, damages the trees, and the knees can sometimes become a problem with lawn-mowers. The seeds are eaten by many different kinds of birds, especially waterfowl.

Bald Cypress belongs to an ancient family that once dominated many prehistoric landscapes. The overall appearance, habitat, and presence of the knees make Bald Cypress one of the most distinctive trees in Texas. The largest tree in our state is probably the state champion Bald Cypress growing near Leakey in Real County. It is 400 inches in circumference, 110 feet tall, and has a crown spread of 100 feet. Bald Cypress is the state tree of Louisiana.

MONTEZUMA CYPRESS. *Taxodium mucronatum.* Ahuehuete, Sabino.

Ahuehuete differs by having nearly evergreen foliage in Texas and is found naturally only in the Rio Grande area in the extreme southern part of the state. In Mexico it is widespread and well known for several huge specimens, most notably the Santa Maria del Tule tree near Oaxaca which has a circumference of 156 feet and stands 126.6 feet tall, and a tree in the Gardens of Chapultepec called the "Cypress of Montezuma" which is 164 feet tall and estimated to be over 700 years old. Resin and pitch from this tree was once used to cure a variety of ailments and was used especially as a dressing for wounds.

Ahuehete has the potential for becoming an outstanding landscape tree. Although it is more open in appearance and lacks the good fall color of regular Bald Cypress, Ahuehuete is faster growing and more drought hardy. This tree has been known to survive 0°F. in Knox City, Texas. The state champion Montezuma Cypress is 45 feet tall, with a trunk circumference of 222 inches and a crown spread of 74 feet. It is growing in Hidalgo County.

5

PONDEROSA PINE

Pinus ponderosa.
Western Yellow Pine.
Impressive tree over 100 feet tall with a narrow open crown and a tall straight trunk to about 2 feet in diameter.

Leaves — Borne in tufts at the ends of the branchlets. Needles usually in clusters of three but sometimes in twos or, rarely, up to five. Dark green when young, older needles yellowish green, 4 to 11 inches long, smell like citrus when crushed.

Flowers — In spring male cones light brown about 1½ inches long near the branch tips. Female cones reddish, almost round, about ¼ inch in length.

Fruit — Ripening in late summer to early fall, often as short-stalked cones 3-5 inches long, light reddish brown, scales with small prickles.

Twigs — Short and stout, orangish at first, becoming dark brown later, having the odor of turpentine when bruised.

Bark — Dark brown to almost black when young, turning reddish brown with age. Deeply furrowed and broken into large irregular plates on older trunks. A faint vanilla smell can often be detected when the nose is placed in the fissures between the plates.

Ponderosa Pine is the most widely distributed pine in North America from Mexico northwestward to British Columbia. In Texas the Ponderosa is confined to woodland habitats in the Davis and Guadalupe mountains, generally at elevations of 4,000 to 8,000 feet. This is the most valuable timber pine in North America but in Texas the trees are generally so widely scattered that they are of little commercial value except for some construction purposes such as the Fort Davis National Historic Site and the Davis Mountain State Park Lodge. Ponderosa Pine has also been utilized for mine timbers, fence posts, and fuel. The wood is usually pale yellow with a reddish brown heartwood and distinct growth rings.

This tree has a long taproot (a four-year-old tree may have a four-foot-long taproot) which makes it drought resistant and windfirm. Its growth rate is moderate but will vary considerably depending on rainfall. These trees are often disfigured or killed by the parasitic Dwarf Mistletoe *(Arceuthobium* sp.) which is Ponderosa Pine's most serious pest. The seeds and the young foliage are important food for many species of wildlife. Indians used the resin of this and other pines to waterproof baskets.

The large pines in the Chisos Mountains of Big Bend National Park, once thought to be Ponderosas, turn out to be *Pinus arizonica* var. *stormiae,* which are primarily Mexican plants, creeping into the U.S. only in this area. The tree once measured as the state champion Ponderosa Pine (105 feet tall, 110-inch trunk circumference, and 48-foot crown spread) is actually this *P. arizonica* var. *stormiae.*

LIMBER PINE. *Pinus strobiformis.*

A slow growing and long-lived small tree found at elevations of 3,500 to 8,500 feet in the Guadalupe and Davis mountains. It differs from the other West Texas pines by regularly having five needles per cluster and 2½ to 10- inch-long cones without prickles on the scales. The seeds are edible but they are smaller and have a thicker shell than Pinyon Pine seeds (see below). The bluish-green needles and light-silvery younger bark make this a pretty pine with ornamental possibilities for dry rocky slopes. Our state champion Limber Pine can be found in the Guadalupe Mountains National Park. It stands 85 feet tall, with a crown spread of 32 feet and a trunk circumference of 108 inches.

MEXICAN PINYON PINE

Pinus cembroides.
Small tree about 30 feet tall with a pyramidal shape when young, becoming rounded with a short stout trunk about 1 foot in diameter.

Leaves — Usually in clusters of three, ¾ to 1¾ inches in length, rich green with a bluish dorsal stripe.

Flowers — Male cones light brown arranged in spirals at the end of the branches; female cones short-stalked, red, also at the end of the branches.

Fruit — Cones maturing late summer to early fall, 1½ inches long, rounded with thick scales and large thick-shelled brown seeds about ½ inch long, edible.

Bark — Deeply furrowed into irregular thick plates with small scaly ridges, gray at first, becoming reddish brown to almost black at maturity.

9

Mexican Pinyon Pine can be found in the southern half of the Trans-Pecos at elevations of 4,400-7,500 feet in shallow rocky or gravelly soils on slopes and canyons. This tree and various Juniper species form large belts of scrub forest at the lower mountain elevations. It is slow growing, long-lived, and the dark bluish-green cast of the needles is fairly distinctive. Young trees are often cut and used locally for

Christmas trees. The soft yellowish wood is used primarily for fuel and fence posts because of its small size. The resin has been used to waterproof baskets and other containers and as a glue; however, the trees' real value lies in the large edible seeds. They are eaten by many species of wildlife and were a staple of the Southwestern Indian diet. Pinyon seeds are sweet when eaten raw but taste best after roasting. In Mexico the seeds are still sold in the markets and can be purchased in many of our own modern market places. They are second only to Pecan in retail value of a wild nut tree crop.

This tree has good ornamental possibilities but the growth is painfully slow and they easily succumb to over-watering. The national champion Mexican Pinyon Pine is 66 feet tall, and has a trunk circumference of 111 inches and a crown spread of 44 feet. It is located at Big Bend National Park in Brewster County.

PAPERSHELL PINYON. *Pinus remota.*

This plant, (formerly *P. cembroides* var. *remota*) differs from *P. cembroides* by having thinner seed shells, usually 2 light green needles per bundle, and an open windswept growth habit. Found growing on the west central portion of the Edwards Plateau, these trees can best be seen in the vicinity of Camp Wood, Leakey, Rocksprings, and north of Brackettville. Pollen records indicate that the range of Pinyon Pine was once more widespread, so perhaps these trees are remnants of an earlier time when the climate was cooler and moister.

Although Papershell Pinyon was once believed to be restricted to the Edwards Plateau, further studies indicate that some of the Pinyon Pines at lower elevations in the Trans-Pecos are also *P. remota* rather than *P. cembroides* as previously thought.

PINYON PINE. *Pinus edulis.*

Usually has 2 dark green needles per bundle, thin-shelled seeds, and larger cones. Although this pine normally occurs farther west, it can be found in Texas in Hudspeth, Culberson, and Deaf Smith counties. It is the state tree of New Mexico.

LOBLOLLY PINE

Pinus taeda.
Tall tree to more than 100 feet with spreading branches forming a compact rounded crown and a long, straight trunk to 2 feet in diameter. Trees growing in the open have a rounded bushy crown with a short stout trunk.

Leaves — Needles almost always in groups of three, 5-9 inches long, light green.

12

Flowers — The yellowish cylindrical male cones are about 1 inch long and arranged in spiral clusters at the end of the branches. The female cones are yellowish, about ½ inch long, also borne at the branch tips.

Fruit — Cones almost cylindrical, 2-6 inches long, not borne on stalks, scales only occasionally armed with prickles, light reddish brown, ripening in the fall.

Twigs — Brown and scaly, terminal buds reddish brown.

Bark — Scaly and nearly black when young, later becoming reddish brown with shallow fissures and broad irregular flaky plates.

Loblolly Pine is the most common pine tree in the forests of East Texas. It is found on almost any site and soil type, generally as a pioneer invading newly cleared areas but will also persist in old growth stands as large specimens. Loblolly Pine is the species that occurs in the Bastrop area as a part of the group often referred to as the "Lost Pines." These trees are actually remnants of a once-contiguous range from East Texas. These pines and some other associated plants can be seen at Bastrop and Buescher State Parks in Bastrop County. The term "loblolly" was originally a seaman's slang used to describe "water gruel or spoonmeal." Later, the name became associated with mudholes

13

and eventually trees growing in low wet areas. Loblolly is one of the most important timber trees in Texas and is widely planted as a tree farm species. The wood is yellowish with a reddish-brown heart. It is coarse grained, resinous with distinct growth rings, and is used for a multitude of purposes, most commonly for lumber, plywood, and pulp.

These trees grow fast (3½ feet in height and ½-inch trunk diameter per year when young, over 60 feet tall in 20 years on good sites) and soon outdistance competing hardwoods. A common scene along roads through the Piney Woods is a tall canopy of Loblolly with a lower level of hardwoods creeping up to replace the pines as they die out. Many species of wildlife feed on the seeds, which are produced in abundance at an early age (trees 10 years old may begin to bear seeds). Unfortunately, Loblolly is very susceptible to fusiform gall rust, and mature trees throughout East Texas are currently being devastated by the southern pine beetle. The good growth rate, attractive form, versatility, and many uses, however, will no doubt perpetuate Loblolly Pine as one of the most widely planted trees in East Texas.

SLASH PINE. *Pinus elliottii.*

Slash Pine is a native of the southeastern states, often planted in East Texas for commercial and ornamental use. It closely resembles Loblolly Pine but differs by having glossy dark brown cones on short stalks and cone scales that are armed with sharp outward curved spines. The state champion Slash Pine is 104 feet tall, with a trunk circumference of 61 inches and a crown spread of 28 feet. It can be found at the E.O. Siecke State Forest near Kirbyville.

SHORTLEAF PINE

Pinus echinata.
Yellow Pine.
Tall tree to 100 feet with a short oval-shaped crown and a long, straight trunk about 1 foot in diameter.

Leaves — Needles usually 2 but sometimes 3 per bundle, 3-5 inches long, yellowish- to dark bluish-green.

Flowers — In spring, male cones yellowish-brown to pale purple about ½ inch long in large clusters at the branch tips; female cones about ½ inch long, single or few per cluster, light red near the ends of the branches.

Fruit — Cones maturing in the fall but persisting on the branches for several years, 1½-2½ inches long, seeds brown to black, about ½ inch long.

Twigs — Stout, brittle, glaucous at first, pale green turning reddish brown with age.

Bark — Reddish brown, broken into thick irregular-shaped scaly plates.

Shortleaf Pine is most frequently found in old fields and upland woods in a variety of soils in the East Texas pine forests from Red River to Grimes and Harris counties. It is an important timber tree; the wood resembles other southern pine woods but is softer and less resinous and is used mostly for pulp, lumber, and plywood. Shortleaf is also a good ornamental pine because it grows fast, is not very susceptible to fusiform rust, and is fairly fire resistant. The thick bark protects the tree from ground fires that would normally kill thinner-barked species. On the other hand, it is susceptible to littleleaf disease, the Nantucket Pine tip moth when it is young, and, as the Loblolly Pine, it is suffering from southern pine beetle attacks. It is a drought-resistant and windfirm tree because of its deep taproot (an 8-foot-tall tree may have a taproot 14 feet long). Shortleaf is the only pine native to Texas that will reliably sprout from the base (up to about 10 years old). Young seedlings about six weeks old usually develop a crook at their base, giving the stem a characteristic J or fishhook shape. The abundant seeds are an important wildlife food. Loblolly and Shortleaf Pines often hybridize, making positive identification difficult where the two are found together. Some authorities believe that the Shortleaf Pine is being absorbed into the Loblolly population through continual hybridization and dilution, with the Loblolly Pine characteristics dominating.

LONGLEAF PINE

Pinus palustris.
A beautiful tree over 100 feet tall with an open, oblong crown and a straight slightly tapering trunk to 2 feet in diameter.

Leaves — Tufted at the end of the branches, typically three dark green needles per bundle, 8 to 18 inches in length, longer than any other native Texas pine.

Flowers — Early to midspring, male cones borne at the tips of the branches, reddish purple, narrowly cylindrical, about 2 inches long; female cones dark purple, about ¼ inch in length at the branch tips.

Fruit — Largest cone of any native pine in Texas, 6 to 10 inches long, almost cylindrical but tapered slightly at the tip, maturing in the fall, seeds about ½ inch long.

Twigs — Stout twigs are terminated by large silvery buds.

Bark — Relatively thin and corky, orangish brown, forming large, irregular, flat plates and fissures on older trees.

Longleaf Pine is a fast growing species found on deep sand-hills in East Texas from Shelby to Trinity, Liberty, Chambers, and Jefferson counties. It is very resistant to fire, with a corky bark and young terminal buds deeply enclosed within the needles for protection. Fires actually contribute to the well-being of these pines by eliminating competition from other species and in controlling a fungal disease (brown spot needle blight) that would otherwise be detrimental. Although once considered catastrophic (particularly by Smokey the Bear), foresters now realize the importance of fire and have incorporated it—in the form of prescribed burns—in the management guidelines for certain species. Some of the most spectacular forests in Texas are almost pure stands of Longleaf where repeated fires have eliminated most of the other species.

Longleaf Pine is one of the finest timber trees east of the rockies. The yellowish wood with a red-brown heartwood is heavy, hard, resinous, and coarse grained with distinct growth rings. It is used for poles, pilings, lumber, masts, and pulp. Longleaf was formerly the world's leading producer of turpentine, rosin, and tar. In the early years of its life, Longleaf Pine exists as a curious tuft of needles, called the "grass stage", showing very little height growth but developing a deep and extensive root system. During this time (3-12 years), it is very resistant to fire damage; however, the thick starchy roots are eagerly uprooted and eaten by wild hogs. When conditions are favorable, growth out of the grass stage is rapid, up to four feet a year.

Longleaf Pine has good ornamental potential because of its stately appearance, attractive foliage, and resistance to fusiform rust and several other problems that normally plague southern pines. The deep taproot makes all but very young plants difficult to transplant. Many species of wildlife feed on the large seeds and the rare red-cockaded woodpecker favors the trunks of mature Longleaf Pine with red heart disease for nesting. Trees that are home to these woodpeckers can often be distinguished by a sticky gum flowing down their trunk. The birds peck the bark to cause this sap flow which creates an irritating barrier discouraging snakes and other predators from entering the nest holes. Alabama-Coushatta Indians use the long needles to weave coil baskets and bowls. The grass stage life cycle, the long needles tufted at the branch tips, and the large cones make this the most distinctive pine tree in Texas. The national champion Longleaf Pine is 125 feet tall and has a trunk circumference of 125 inches and a crown spread of 63 feet. It is located in Boykin Springs State Recreational Area in Jasper County.

DOUGLAS FIR

Pseudotsuga menziesii.
Evergreen tree with a compact, conical crown, attaining a height of 80 feet in Texas.

Pinaceae - Pine Family

Leaves — Flat, linear, tip blunt or pointed, 1 inch long, bluish green; borne singly from the branch (not in bundles) on a short narrow petiole; leaves arranged spirally around the branch, but somewhat flattened into two ranks on either side of the branches.

Flowers — The male cones are oblong, reddish, scattered along the branches; female cones terminal or in upper leaf axils. Both sexes found on the same tree.

Fruit — The cones are reddish brown, 2-4 inches long, oblong or ovoid, hanging downward from the branch; the cone has distinctive 3-pointed bracts extending beyond the scales.

Twigs — Slender, orange at first, becoming gray-brown.

Bark — Young trees have smooth, gray bark with resin blisters, later becoming thick and furrowed with age.

In Texas, the Douglas Fir is found growing only in the high, canyon areas of the Chisos and Guadalupe mountains of West Texas. It also occurs in Mexico, and extends northwestward to British Columbia. The Douglas Fir is considered one of the most important timber trees in the U.S. and possibly worldwide. Reaching heights up to 250 feet in the northwest, it is one of the tallest in the U.S., outranked only by the Giant Sequoia and the Redwood. Douglas Fir wood is highly valued for its strength and durability. It is used for structural beams, bridges, docks, and in shipbuilding.

22

The arching beams over the roof of the Mormon Tabernacle are of Douglas Fir, and miles and miles of railroad track in the West are laid on ties made of it. Because it is strong but light and does not warp, it is used for plywood and paneling.

The Douglas Fir is a very long-lived tree (500 to 1000 years). Due to its fast growth and attractive shape, it makes good Christmas trees and is prized as an ornamental. The Douglas Fir trees of Texas are considered to be members of the Rocky Mountain variety, *Pseudotsuga menziesii* var. *glauca.* These trees are distinguished by having a smaller cone, bluish-colored leaves, and a more compact stature.

ARIZONA CYPRESS

Cupressus arizonica.
Cedro.
An evergreen tree with a conical crown and a straight trunk usually growing up to 70 feet tall.

Leaves — Scalelike, pointed blue green with a whitish bloom, aromatic.

Flowers — Borne in spring, male cones very small, female cones green, erect. Male and female cones borne on the same tree at the tips of the branches.

Fruit — Cone, ¾ to 1¼ inches across, hard, woody, made up of flattened scales with a stout point in center, gray to

reddish brown, maturing the second year, often persisting several years, seeds oblong to triangular.
Twigs — Stiff, gray, four-angled.
Bark — Smooth, thin, and splitting into thin narrow strips exposing the reddish-brown inner bark, or on some older trees turning gray to dark brown or blackish and breaking into irregular plates.

This magnificent tree is native to Texas only in the high wooded area of the Chisos Mountains of Big Bend National Park. It is also found in northern Mexico and ranges westward to southern California. The population of Arizona Cypress in Texas is thought to be remnants of the Pleistocene era when the climate was much cooler and wetter. Very likely these trees were once more widespread in Texas but now remain only in the isolated and protected canyons of the Chisos Mountains.

The Arizona Cypress has blue-gray, juniper-like foliage, quite aromatic when crushed. It is a compact, fast-growing tree cultivated for Christmas trees in the West. Arizona Cypress is used in shelterbelts and sometimes planted on slopes for erosion control. It is long-lived and very drought tolerant. Because of its attractiveness, it is widely planted as an ornamental. The wood is heavy and occasionally used for fence posts and mine timbers. Our state champion Arizona Cypress can be found in Big Bend National Park; it measures 112 feet tall, with a trunk circumference of 134 inches and a crown spread of 32 feet.

ALLIGATOR JUNIPER

Juniperus deppeana.
Evergreen tree to 50-60 feet with widespreading branches and a thick, low trunk. Easily distinguished by its checkered bark.

Leaves — Bluish green, scalelike, ⅛ inch long, in opposite pairs; thickly dotted with resin.

Flowers — Male and female cones on separate trees. Male cones fleshy, ⅛ inch long at the ends of the branchlet; female cones small, oval, composed of scales.

Fruit — Berry-like cone, reddish brown, ½ inch across; maturing the second year.

26

Twigs — Four-angled, pale blue-green turning reddish brown with age.

Bark — Gray to reddish brown, rough, ¼ inch thick, deeply furrowed into checkered or square-plated bark.

The Alligator Juniper is found growing scattered on dry hillsides and oak woodland areas of West Texas and adjacent Mexico at altitudes of 4,500 to 8,000 feet. It also grows in New Mexico and Arizona. This tree is easily recognized by the rough square-plated or checkered bark, resembling the hide of an alligator—quite noticeable, even from a distance. The Alligator Juniper is a very long-lived tree (up to 500–800 years). It is slow growing and very drought resistant. The light reddish wood is soft and brittle, and occasionally used for fuel and fence posts. The Alligator Juniper can become a range and forest pest in some areas; when cut, it will readily sprout from the stump.

The Juniper fruit is eaten by many types of wildlife including birds, fox, squirrel, and black bear. The leaves are sometimes browsed by deer and are reportedly used in Mexico as a treatment for rheumatism. Because of its widespreading crown and interestingly textured bark, the Alligator Juniper is a desirable ornamental. It is actually more popular overseas, and many cultivars have been developed in Australia.

DROOPING JUNIPER

Juniperus flaccida.
Weeping Juniper.
An evergreen shrub or tree to 30 feet with a wide-spreading crown of pendant branchlets.

Leaves — Scalelike, ⅛ inch long, overlapping, pressed against the branchlets; often gland dotted.

Flowers — Male and female cones on separate plants. Male cones small, cylinder-shaped at the tips of branchlets; female cones small, ovoid.

Fruit — Berry-like cones, ⅓ to ⅝ inch across; reddish brown.

Twigs — Drooping; slim with reddish brown, loosely scaly bark.

Bark — Reddish brown with thin, narrow scales.

The Drooping Juniper is primarily native to Mexico and creeps into the U.S. only in the Chisos Mountains of Texas' Big Bend National Park. This tree is readily distinguished from all other junipers by its drooping or pendant branchlets, giving it a graceful, almost wilted, appearance. Drooping Juniper is found on dry, rocky sites of canyons, hillsides, and ridges. According to some of the older ranchers in the Big Bend area, the Drooping Juniper was formerly more common there. A large number were supposedly cut for timbering the mines of Boquillas, Mexico. The wood is also used for fence posts.

The Juniper fruit is eaten by a wide variety of wildlife species. As with most other Juniper species, this plant is slow growing, long-lived, and very drought resistant. Drooping Juniper has been cultivated as an ornamental in southern Europe and northern Africa. The national champion is in Big Bend National Park, and measures 55 feet tall with a trunk circumference of 102 inches and shades an area 35 feet across.

ASHE JUNIPER

Juniperus ashei.
Mountain Cedar, Enebro, Sabino.
Evergreen shrub or tree up to 25 feet.
Grows in rocky limestone hills and
canyons of Central and West Texas.

Leaves — Scalelike, dark green or blue green, less than .1 inch
long; on seedling plants and new growth the leaves are
awl-shaped and sharp pointed.

Flowers — Male and female cones on separate plants, minute; male cones oblong, female cones ovoid with leathery scales.
Fruit — Berry-like cone, ¼ to ⅜ inch across, bluish, thick skinned; fruits in the fall.
Twigs — Reddish, scaly.
Bark — Gray to reddish brown, becomes shaggy and shredding with age. Occasionally, white to gray patches are seen on the bark which are caused by a type of lichen.

Ashe Juniper is the dominant juniper of the Texas Hill Country and is commonly referred to as "cedar." Its name, Ashe Juniper, honors William W. Ashe, a botanist and forester from North Carolina. The Juniper wood is durable and resistant to decay and therefore used extensively for fence posts and fuel. From 1902 to 1940, chopping cedar was a major source of livelihood for many people, and even today there are still a few "cedar choppers" making a living from this resource. Unlike many other Juniper species, this plant is resistant to cedar apple rust. It has an invasive nature and can form impenetrable thickets inhibiting the growth of grasses and other herbaceous plants, and is often looked on as a pest and eradicated.

It is probable that the Ashe Juniper was once primarily confined to canyons and brakes, but due to overgrazing and the elimination of natural fires, it has spread throughout the Hill Country. Once it is cut or burned, however, it will not resprout from the base. Many people are allergic to the infamous "cedar" pollen and dread the winter months when the male trees are pollinating. The female trees bear the cone or "berry" and cause no harm to the sinuses. In Mexico, the ashes of this juniper bark are reportedly used in the preparation of lime for making corn tortillas.

The Ashe Juniper fruit is eaten by a number of birds and mammals, and the tree provides cover for deer and other wildlife. There is a small black and yellow bird, appropriately called the golden-cheeked warbler, which spends the winter in Central America, then migrates to Texas to nest among older stands of the Ashe Juniper. It utilizes the strips of bark from the mature trees in its nest building. Although somewhat elusive, the warbler can be seen or heard from March to May in certain canyon areas of the Texas Hill Country near these stands of Ashe Juniper and Texas Red Oak.

ONE-SEED JUNIPER. *Juniperus monosperma.*

This multi-branched juniper found in the northern plains country and the Trans-Pecos is similar to *J. ashei* but has a smaller bluish-black to rust-colored cone or "berry." One-Seed Juniper ranges northward to Nevada and westward to northern Arizona, and is the most prevalent juniper seen in New Mexico. The wood has been used by the Navahos for prayer sticks, war bows, and as charcoal for smelting their silver jewelry.

REDBERRY JUNIPER. *Juniperus pinchotii.*

Redberry Juniper is a shrub or multi-branched tree to 20 feet which grows in dry, rocky hillsides and canyon areas in the western part of the Edwards Plateau, the Trans-Pecos, and the Panhandle. It is distinguished from Ashe Juniper by having red fruit and more erect branching. This Juniper sprouts readily from the base after it is cut or burned. Palo Duro Canyon gets its name from the "hard wood" of this plant which grows in abundance in that area.

EASTERN RED CEDAR

Juniperus virginiana.
Evergreen shrub or tree to 50 feet with a dense pyramidal crown and an often fluted trunk up to two feet in diameter.

Leaves — Scalelike, dark green, 1/16 inch long. With or without a rounded gland on the back. On young vigorous new growth the leaves are longer and needle-like.

Flowers — Males and female flowers borne on separate trees at the ends of the twigs. Male trees often appear golden due to the yellow pollen produced in the oval catkins. Female cones spherical.

33

Fruit — Berry-like cone, pale blue, ¼ to ⅜ inch across with a dry resinous pulp.
Twigs — Rounded or four-angled, reddish brown.
Bark — Reddish brown, thin, peeling off in long shredlike strips.

Eastern Red Cedar is found growing primarily on dry hill-sides, along fence rows, under power lines, and sometimes near creeks in East Texas west to about Wichita, Williamson, and Caldwell counties. This tree has become somewhat well known for its beautiful fragrant wood which has a red heartwood with a white sapwood. Eastern Red Cedar's attractive nature and reputed insect-repelling properties have made it popular for cabinetmaking, paneling, novelty items, as linings for closets, and for the renowned cedar chests where clothes can be kept without fear of insect damage. The wood is very resistant to decay and makes good fence posts. Baton Rouge (Red Stick), Louisiana, gets its name from the red wood of this tree.

Due to its nice appearance and uniform shape, this cedar is locally popular for Christmas trees and is often planted as an ornamental. Many horticultural cultivars have been developed based on size, shape, and foliage color. It can harbor cedar apple rust, however, and care should be taken not to plant it near an apple orchard. The fruit is eaten by many birds and mammals. An extract of cedar oil is used in medicines and perfumes, and a reddish dye can be obtained from the root and bark.

SOUTHERN RED CEDAR. *Juniperus silicicola.*
Coast Juniper, Sand Cedar.

Southern Red Cedar looks very similar to Eastern Red Cedar but has somewhat pendant or hanging branches and a smaller cone or "berry." It is found in moist, sandy soils in Southeast Texas west to about Jackson County. The state champion Southern Red Cedar is 75 feet tall and has a trunk girth of 61 inches and a crown spread of 26 feet. It is located at the Robert A. Vines Research Center in Houston.

ROCKY MOUNTAIN JUNIPER. *Juniperus scopulorum.*

This tree is very similar in appearance to Eastern Red Cedar but has pale, light green or bluish foliage and larger fruit that takes two years to mature. This plant is found on rocky hillsides and canyons in the Guadalupe Mountains and the Texas Panhandle, and ranges north into British Columbia. It is used in reforestation projects and shelterbelt plantings. Though the wood is as attractive as that of the Eastern Red Cedar, the trunks are not as straight and tall and the tree, therefore, has little timber value but is often used for novelty items available at most southwestern tourist shops.

SALT CEDAR

Tamarix sp.
Tamarisk.

Coniferous-looking, evergreen, flowering tree 20-30 feet tall with an irregular, upright, oval crown of drooping branches often brushing the ground and usually dividing into several low-branching trunks.

Leaves — Scalelike and tiny up to ⅛ inch long and hugging the twig, gray or bluish green.

Flowers — In the summer off the new wood, very small but in showy tight clusters, pink or white, 5-parted with 5 stamens.

Fruit — Tiny capsules usually less than ⅛ inch long dividing into 3-5 parts and containing many minute seeds.

Twigs — Very thin and supple, red brown and smooth at first, becoming darker and rougher with age.

Bark — Smooth and thin when young, ultimately developing thick, blocky flat-topped ridges.

Salt Cedar is a familiar evergreen tree along waterways and near old homesteads throughout West and Southwest Texas. Originally from the Mediterranean area, most species were introduced by the United States Department of Agriculture from about 1899 to 1915, intended for erosion control and windbreaks, but they have escaped and now dominate some areas of the Rio Grande River. They are excellent, fast-growing shade trees for brackish or dry areas where little else will survive, and provide some welcome relief for a region almost devoid of trees. Wildlife use the plants for cover and nesting.

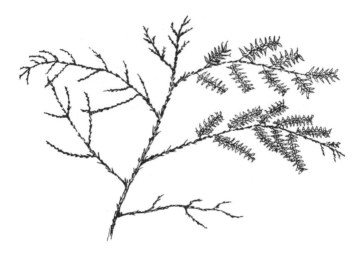

Salt Cedars are considered pestiferous because they choke up small waterways and crowd out more desirable native vegetation. Their roots rival Mesquite in deeply searching for groundwater which it sucks out voraciously. The fallen leaves give the soil a high salt content, inhibiting the growth of other plants and creating a sterile situation. Once established they are difficult to eradicate as they sprout readily. A more favorable note is that honeybees make good use of the abundant summer flowers. The national champion *Tamarix gallica* is growing in the Big Bend National Park. It is 64 feet tall, has a trunk circumference of 128 inches, and covers an area 66 feet across.

SABAL PALM

Sabal mexicana. [Sabal texana].
Rio Grande Palmetto, Palma de Micharos.
A native Texas palm to 50 feet with large fan-shaped leaves forming a rounded crown.

Leaves — Fan-shaped, green, 5-7 feet long and equally as wide. Leaf stem stiff, half-rounded, equally as long as or longer than the blade, lacking prickles.

Flowers — Stalks 6-8 feet long in drooping clusters. Flowers small, white or greenish.

Fruit — Dull black, rounded, often lobed, ½ to ¾ inch across; pulp dry, sweet, edible; seed dark brown and shiny, one edge often flattened.

Bark — Reddish brown, leaf scars prominent, leaf bases cling to trunk, forming a distinctive cross-hatch appearance, and often shed with age.

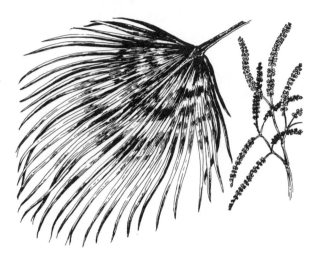

The Sabal Palm is the only tree-sized palm native to Texas. It is found at the very southern tip of the state along resacas and flatlands near the lower Rio Grande River and in Mexico. In Texas, the Sabal is now considered quite rare in nature. According to the early accounts, the Sabal Palm was at one time more widespread in Texas and Mexico. Arthur Schott, of the first Mexico-United States boundary survey in the early 1800's, reported that the palm extended along the Rio Grande up to about 80 miles from the Gulf, and occupied approximately 40,000 acres. Today, due to extensive land clearing in the Lower Rio Grande Valley, only a 32-acre Sanctuary and a few acres on private property of the Sabal Palm forest remain intact. The Sabal Palm Grove Sanctuary is owned and operated by the National Audubon Society. With its associated flora and fauna, this palm comprises a unique subtropical community. Other plants of the palm grove include Texas Ebony, Tepeguaje, Anaqua, and

David's Milkberry, a tropical vine at the northernmost extent of its range.

The palm forest also supports some interesting wildlife. Several bird species which range just north of the Rio Grande River include the green jay, plain chachalaca, buff-bellied hummingbird, and the white-tipped dove. Two endangered cats in Texas—the ocelot and the jaguarundi—are known to take cover periodically in the palm forest. The drooping palm leaves even provide a roosting habitat for two species of subtropical bat—the Southern Yellow Bat and a rare variety of the Northern Yellow Bat. The Sabal Palm has other uses as well: The thick trunks have been used as wharf pilings along the Gulf, and the fronds are sometimes used as thatching for houses. The fruit of the palm, called *micharos,* are sold in Mexican markets.

Although rare in the wild in Texas, the Sabal Palm is widely cultivated as an ornamental. While the wild plants grow somewhat slowly, those in cultivation have fast growth rates. The Sabal can be seen throughout South Texas and is hardy up to Austin; however, to truly capture the essence of this tree, one must see them in their natural habitat. For information on the sanctuary write to: Sabal Palm Grove Sanctuary, National Audubon Society, P.O. Box 8277, Brownsville, Texas 78520.

Isolated populations of trunked Sabals reaching almost 20 feet tall can be found scattered across the state's eastern coastal plain. The most notable group is located about eight miles west of Brazoria in Brazoria County. These are considered by various authorities to be either trunked forms of *Sabal minor,* hybrids between *S. minor* and *S. mexicana,* or an independent species.

PETTICOAT PALM

Washingtonia filifera.
Washingtonia Palm.

A medium-sized tree to 35 feet tall with a narrow columnar habit and a tufted rounded crown about 12 feet wide. Often with a skirt of dead leaves shielding the trunk.

Leaves — Evergreen and crowded at the tip of the trunk, the deeply cut, finger-like, fan-shaped leaves are 3 to 4 feet in diameter and borne on stout petioles 3 to 4 feet long with sharp spines on the margins. Each finger segment bears abundant threads or filaments on the margins.

41

Flowers — Borne in early to midsummer in drooping clusters up to 12 feet in length containing numerous small white flowers about ¼ inch across.

Fruit — Ripening in late summer or early fall, dark blue or almost black, thin-fleshed single seed, rounded, ⅓ or more inch in diameter. The light brown or tan hard seed is slightly smaller than the mature fruit.

Bark — Green at first, becoming reddish brown where the dead leaves are removed, maturing into a thick, scaly, tight, usually gray skin marked with vertical cracks and ridges.

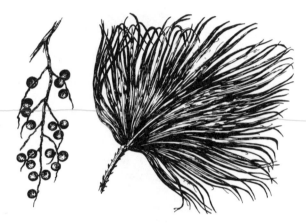

Petticoat Palms are native to oases and canyons in the more arid areas of southern California, western Arizona and northern Mexico. In Texas they are planted and reseed themselves in urban areas from about San Antonio south to Brownsville. Their natural range is rather restricted but these palms are widely planted as ornamentals throughout the warmer areas of the world. In cultivation they are distinguished tall palms at their best, with a handsome shag or "petticoat" of dead leaves covering the trunk almost to the ground. Within their natural range they were important to the local Indians: The leaves were used for thatch, the fruit, seeds, and the cabbage-like heart of the growing tip for food.

Palms in general give a tropical, almost prehistoric look to a landscape. They are among the seven oldest known flowering plant families. Petticoats are the largest, hardy fan palms grown out of doors in Texas. They sometimes get a fatal crown rot here and the thatch of leaves can harbor wasps and rodents as well as desirable songbirds.

WASHINGTONIA PALM. *Washingtonia filifera* var. *robusta*.

An ornamental planted throughout South Texas. It differs from the species by being taller, with a thinner trunk and few filaments on the leaf margins. A general rule of thumb for the field observer is that *robusta* keeps its leaves green as they lie to the trunk, whereas *filifera* leaves are green only halfway to the point of lying against the trunk. Most filiferas were killed by the 1983 freeze and persist as stark trunks against the landscape.

GIANT YUCCA

Yucca faxoniana.
[*Yucca carnerosana.*] Faxon Yucca.
A handsome broadleaf tree Yucca,
usually with a single or occasionally
branched stem to about 20 feet tall
with a stout trunk 1 foot in diameter.

Leaves — Alternate, persistent 3-4 feet long and 2-3 inches wide
and usually clustered near the heads but live leaves may
extend down the trunk for some distance, dark yellow-
green with filamentous margins, smooth on both surfaces and armed with a short stout spine tip.

44

Flowers — Usually borne in late spring but in nature may be found throughout the growing season in tall terminal rounded branched clusters up to 7 feet tall with hundreds of white, somewhat fleshy, 3-inch perfect flowers consisting of 6 stamens and 6 petal-like segments. The entire infloresence is usually held only about a foot above the leaf clusters.

Fruit — Maturing in early fall as 3- to 4-inch-long leathery capsules, rounded at the base and tapering to an abrupt point, containing many triangular thin black seeds.

Bark — At first covered with a loose dense thatch of the persistent dead leaves that result in narrow lateral scars and eventually turn dark gray to almost black, breaking into narrow vertical fissures with broad roughened ridges.

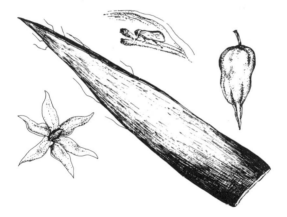

Giant Yucca is the largest Texas species and grows most commonly in the Big Bend country of Brewster County and throughout the Dead Horse Mountains. On foothills and lower mountain slopes they often form open forests that are spectacular when in bloom. They are striking ornamentals and in West Texas have been used by the Highway Department for roadside plantings. The broadleaf tree Yuccas were used extensively by the southwestern Indians and Mexicans for many purposes. The flowers were a favorite food, especially good when fried with eggs. Palisade construction was often made out of the trunks and in times of drought the flower stalks were fed to cattle. Immature fruits are edible either raw, pickled, boiled, or roasted. The fibers of the Yucca leaves were used in making cordage or twine for necessities such as nets, snares, blankets, and sandals. In Mexico today, the leaf fibers of Giant Yucca and *Agave lechegilla,* known as "ixtle" or "Palma ixtle," are commercially harvested and sold for making rope, twine, saddle blankets, mats, and rugs. This area in northern Mexico is known locally as Zona Ixtlera.

One of the most fascinating relationships between plant and insect exist between Yuccas and the Yucca Moth (*Pronuba* sp.). Each is completely dependent on the other for reproduction. The moth lays her eggs in the flower ovary and then deliberately pollinates the flower by placing rolled up balls of pollen on the stigma. This insures pollination and food for the moth larvae in the developing seeds. Gently shake the flower stalk of any *Yucca* sp. and observe the small woolly white moths fly out. The national champion Giant Yucca (Hudspeth County) is 25 feet tall with a crown spread of 10 feet and a trunk circumference of 51 inches.

Recent studies indicate that the true *Yucca carnerosanas* only occur in Mexico, and that the Texas plants formerly called *Y. carnerosana* are actually *Y. faxoniana.*

SPANISH DAGGER

Yucca treculeana.
Trecul Yucca.
Spanish Dagger can ultimately reach 20 feet in height, usually with several somewhat symmetrical heads or trunks. The "coastal" form tends to get taller with shorter leaves and a relatively slender trunk whereas the "inland" form has longer leaves with a shorter, stockier trunk.

Leaves — Thick, dark green or bluish green, usually clustered near the tips of the trunks but vigorous shoots may have live leaves all the way to the base. Deeply concave up to

47

40 inches long and 3 inches wide at the base, tapering to a stout spine tip. The margins are generally without peeling fibers; the lower surface is rough to the touch at least towards the tip but the upper surface is relatively smooth.

Flowers — Borne in early to midspring in dense terminal panicles up to 3 feet tall and 2 feet broad. Individual flowers are almost spherical, drooping, cream colored, perfect with 6 tepals up to 2 inches long and 6 stamens.

Fruit — Maturing in the fall as leathery cylindrical capsules up to 4 inches long filled with tightly-packed, black, flat triangular seeds about ½ inch wide.

Bark — Dark gray to almost black, at first with thin lateral scars of the old leaf bases, later becoming roughened and splitting into narrow fissures or small silvery scales. Often covered with a sheath of persistent dead leaves loosely lying flat against the trunk.

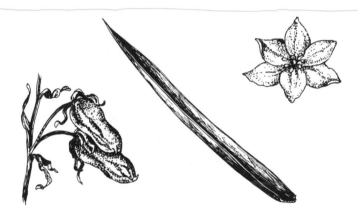

Spanish Dagger is usually found along roadsides, fence lines, in brushland, and at the edge of woods from the southern part of the Edwards Plateau south throughout the Rio Grande Plains. This is one of our most beautiful Yuccas and occasionally is grown as an ornamental in Europe. Yuccas are often planted as accent specimens but the arborescent species should not be overlooked as small flowering trees. The most common mistake made when using Yuccas in the landscape is to plant them too close to a walk or driveway where they become a nuisance and have to be removed or have the spiny leaf tips cut off making them look ridiculous.

Indians had many uses for Yuccas. The trunks were used for stockades and, along with the leaves, as a source of coarse fiber used for mats, cloth, rope, sandals, baskets, and paper. A soap was made from the roots, known as *amole,* which was used for washing clothes and hair. Young flower stalks, buds, and the flowers themselves can be eaten raw, boiled, or pickled. The seeds are considered to have laxative properties. Leaves were used in thatching huts, and natives used the sharp spine tips to puncture snake bite wounds in order to release the poison.

Yuccas in general are not particularly useful to wildlife, but doves and mockingbirds seem to favor the arborescent species as nesting sites.

TORREY YUCCA. *Yucca torreyi.*

Torrey Yucca can be readily distinguished from the other broadleaf Yuccas by its more erect leaves and asymmetrical, rather untidy, appearance. Some individuals have a very marked bluish tinge to the leaves. It is the most common arborescent Yucca in West Texas east to about the Junction and Uvalde areas. Deer and cattle frequently browse the flowers. This was one of the most important sources of fiber to the West Texas Indians who also ate the leathery capsules, either raw or roasted, and boiled the dried flowers for a tea and as a cough remedy. Torrey Yucca will hybridize with *Yucca treculeana* and *Yucca faxoniana* where their ranges overlap.

THOMPSON YUCCA

Yucca thompsoniana.
Small narrow-leaf Yucca up to 10 feet tall, usually with a tidy appearance but occasionally somewhat asymmetrical with one to several heads.

Leaves — Alternate, but usually tightly clustered at the tips of each head, persistent, 10-18 inches long and 1 / 2 inch or less wide. Yellowish to bluish green with a thin yellow margin roughened with tiny teeth and tipped with a small slender spine.

Flowers — Late spring in terminal clusters about 3 feet tall containing many perfect bright white flowers with 6 tepals, 6 stamens, and a single three-lobed ovary. Individual flowers are somewhat fleshy and about 1¾ inches long.

Fruit — Maturing late summer to early fall as many dry three-lobed capsules about 2 inches or so long, and about ⅓ to ¼ of that length tapering into long points. Each of the 3 lobes contain many black triangular flat seeds about ¼ inch wide.

Bark — Trunks usually covered by a sheath of downward-pointing, appressed dead leaves that eventually result in closely-packed, thin horizontal leaf scars. Very old trunks are dark gray and roughened or with small scales peeling at the edges.

Thompson Yucca is probably the most common thin-leaved tree Yucca species occurring in the lower mountain elevations of the Trans-Pecos. It is a popular ornamental in Texas and is widely planted throughout drier portions of the state. The trees are prized for their attractive foliage and compact symmetrical appearance. Cultivated specimens sometimes have their skirt of dead leaves removed, making them look as naked and silly as a plucked chicken. Indians used the thin-leaved Yucca species in much the same ways as the thick-leaved ones—the flowers for food, the leaves for thatch and fiber, and the roots as a soap substitute. The Yucca moths (*Pronuba* sp.) also use this tree as a nursery, as described for the Giant Yucca.

Doves and mockingbirds frequently build their nests in these and other tree Yucca species. Many insect and small animal species benefit from the microcosmic world of

51

shelter these trees provide from an otherwise hostile environment. Yucca flowers have such perfect symmetry they served as the example for the popular plastic models seen in science classes.

BEAKED YUCCA. *Yucca rostrata.*

Beaked Yucca is a thin-leaved tree Yucca growing to almost 15 feet tall, with one to several heads of bluish- or sometimes yellowish-green leaves armed with a small spine tip. The margins are yellow and smooth without tiny teeth or filamentous hairs. It is a beautiful Yucca and sometimes cultivated in other parts of the state but in nature is found only in southern Brewster County and adjacent northern Mexico.

SOAPTREE YUCCA. *Yucca elata.*
Palmella.

A thin-leaved tree Yucca found on grasslands, dry hills, and washes at lower elevations of the Trans-Pecos mountains. It differs from other thin-leaved tree Yuccas by having filamentous leaf margins and the leaves with a slight keel of tiny teeth on the underside. Indians ate the flowers and the young flower stalks which resemble large asparagus. They also used the foliage for fiber and thatch. Navaho Indians used the soapy extract from the roots for washing wool prior to weaving their fine blankets and rugs. Soaptree Yucca is the state flower of New Mexico.

GINKGO

Ginkgo biloba.
Maidenhair Tree.
Medium sized deciduous tree about 60 feet tall with a somewhat asymmetric narrow crown and a relatively thin trunk 18 inches thick.

Leaves — First-year tip growth is a series of widely spaced alternate nodes which later develop into spur shoots bearing from 2-16 leaves in three spirally-arranged clusters. Each fan-shaped leaf is 1 to 2 inches in length and 1½ to 3 inches across, conspicuously parallel veined, bright green on both surfaces turning yellow when going deciduous in the fall.

53

Flowers — Borne in the spring as the leaves unfold, the sexes on separate trees. Male structures from the spur shoots in clusters resembling 1-inch-long greenish catkins, the female portions also arising from spur shoots as two minute ovules on slender stalks about 1 inch long.

Fruit — Maturing in late summer or early fall on the female trees as ¾ inch long yellowish egg-shaped seeds covered with a relatively thin, somewhat ill-smelling flesh.

Twigs — Green and smooth when young, turning stiff yellowish to light brown when older. The numerous corky spur shoots with the small scaly terminal buds are quite distinctive.

Bark — Fairly thick, yellowish light brown, and loosely scaly when young, becoming gray and irregularly fissured with age.

Ginkgo is the sole surviving member of an ancient order of plants related to pines and cycads that formerly flourished across North America, Europe, and Asia. Today their natural range is limited to small isolated populations in remote regions of western China. Before their wild populations were discovered, the Ginkgo was known only from fossil specimens and living trees planted around Buddhist temples where they had been cultivated as sacred trees since about the eighth century A.D. They have become widely planted throughout the temperate parts of the world and are one of the most popular street and shade trees in some parts of North America. In Texas, they do best planted in the northern and eastern parts of the state in areas of good drainage.

The Ginkgo is known for its lack of insect pest or disease problems, ability to withstand city air pollution, and easy cultivation. Female trees are usually frowned upon because of the stench given off by the ripe fruits, so most nurseries offer grafted male stock. Despite the foul-smelling flesh, the seed inside was relished by Orientals for its sweet and resinous flavor. The seed is also said to help digestion and minimize the effects of alcohol. The inner bark can be used to dye cloth light brown. Ginkgo has long been used medicinally. Researchers say that extract of Ginkgo increases oxygenation of the brain, improves peripheral circulation and may have use in treating senility, memory loss, and tinitus (ringing of the ears).

Ginkgos grow slowly and do not begin to bear seeds until they are about 30 years old. They are somewhat gawky looking when young and do not develop their true crown shape until almost mature. There are very few Ginkgos in Texas that are even close to 100 years old. A nice specimen Ginkgo over 100 years old stands on the grounds of Tyler City Hall. It was brought from Japan by Ambassador Richard Bennett Hubbard and planted in Tyler in 1889. Despite being struck by lightning some years ago the tree is in good health.

BLACK WILLOW

Salix nigra.
A rapid growing tree usually to 40 feet tall, often multi-trunked with an irregular crown.

Leaves — Blades 3-6 inches long and ¼ to ¾ inch wide with finely toothed margins. Turning yellow in fall.
Flowers — Yellow catkins, about 1 inch in length borne in early spring. The male and female flowers are on separate plants.
Fruit — Light brown capsule ¼ inch or less in length, maturing in late spring and early summer, containing many minute seeds covered with silky hairs.

56

Twigs — Reddish brown, the buds covered by a single caplike
   scale.
Bark — Brown to black, deeply fissured, flat ridges dividing into
   thick scales; becoming somewhat shaggy with age.

Black Willow is the largest and most widespread Texas willow species. It is found along river banks, drainage ditches,
swamps, and in wet soil throughout the state. The willow
is fast-growing, averaging 4 feet of growth in one year. It is
a weak tree, subject to breakage, and has a relatively short
life span. The extensive shallow roots are known to break
pavement and clog drains. This same property makes the
willow useful in erosion control; the dense network of roots
helps to stabilize the soil. Black Willow wood is soft, light,
and weak. It is used for boxes, artificial limbs, fuel, and, during revolutionary times, for the manufacture of a high grade
of charcoal for black gunpowder. The wood is flexible and
used for weaving baskets, wicker furniture, and effective
disciplinary switches. Willow branches are also used as

57

divining rods to locate water. The Indians made an infusion of the bark to alleviate fever and aches. Willow bark does, in fact, contain salicylic acid which is present in aspirin.

This tree roots easily from cuttings: One can take a live willow branch, press it into the mud, and watch it grow.

SOUTHWESTERN BLACK WILLOW. *Salix gooddingii.*

Moderate sized trees 30 feet tall or more, found near water in the western third of the state. It differs from Black Willow by having leaves with green undersides and yellow twigs.

PEACH-LEAF WILLOW, *Salix amygdaloides.*

An attractive small tree to about 30 feet tall found in the Panhandle and Trans-Pecos areas of Texas. The leaves are about 2-5 inches in length and are yellow green above with whitish undersides. The light-colored undersides give the plant a beautiful effect when blown by a slight breeze.

ARROYO WILLOW. *Salix lasiolepis.*

A shrub or small tree to barely 20 feet tall with narrow leaves 3-6 inches in length and up to 1 inch wide, dark green above and densely covered with whitish hairs beneath. It is found near water in the western third of Texas.

CAROLINA WILLOW. *Salix caroliniana.*

This is a small tree to 20 feet tall with narrow leaves up to 5 inches long and ½ to 1 inch wide. The leaves are dark green above and covered with a whitish bloom beneath. It is found primarily along rocky waterways in the Edwards Plateau and South Central Texas. These are the common willows with whitish undersides that can be found in Lost Maples State Natural Area.

EASTERN COTTONWOOD

Populus deltoides.
Alamo.
Large deciduous tree over 100 feet tall, breaking into many large branches to form a broad open crown and a stout trunk 3 feet or more in diameter.

Leaves — Alternate, borne on a long petiole 2-3 inches in length, roughly triangular 3-7 inches long and about as wide. Shiny green on top, lighter green below.

Flowers — Male and female flowers on separate trees in early spring. Male flowers about 2 inches long and females up to 4 inches in length when mature.

59

Fruit — Capsules maturing in late spring – early summer, in long drooping racemes, with many seeds in each pod. Each tiny seed has a tuft of cottony hairs which enables it to drift for long distances in the wind.

Twigs — Yellowish brown at first, turning light gray later. Leaf scars prominent, giving the twigs a roughened appearance. The scaly winter buds are long, pointed, cone-shaped, and shiny brown, the glossy terminal bud almost an inch in length.

Bark — Smooth and thin at first, yellowish gray becoming ashy gray and deeply furrowed with rounded ridges later.

Cottonwood is almost an aquatic plant, rarely found far from water throughout the eastern half of the state west to about Wilbarger, Runnels, and Uvalde counties. It is considered a pioneer species that quickly invades disturbed soils or new sand bars. The trees are extremely fast growing and on good sites can easily average up to 5 feet of height growth annually the first 25 years. On poor sites they are invariably attacked by a host of pests and diseases, often causing them to suddenly drop large branches or die completely. Cottonwood seed is viable for only a short time and must find wet soil or die in a few days, but the trees are easily propagated by cuttings. Their fast growth once caused Cottonwoods to be frequently planted as street and shade trees, but this is now generally discouraged because the wide-spreading shallow roots clog drains and lift up pavement and they are relatively short-lived (about 30-60 years reliably). Some cities even have ordinances prohibiting their planting.

As an ornamental, the tree does have a place planted near a stream or pond (use male or "cottonless varieties") where they can soon develop into a substantial tree that offers more than the solemn dark shade of a large oak tree. The long petioled leaves flutter in the slightest breeze, giving a light shade, reflecting flashes of sunlight, and making sounds as restive as waves at the beach. Cottonwood has a whitish sapwood with a grayish heart and inconspicuous growth rings. It is light, soft, and has an unpleasant odor when wet. Some of the best book and magazine paper is made from Cottonwood pulp and it is also used for pallet lumber and food containers such as berry boxes.

The foliage, bark, seeds, and leaves are all important to wildlife. Early settlers welcomed the sight of Cottonwoods for it meant water was nearby. The famous mission Alamo in San Antonio bears the Spanish name for these trees that were growing along the river. The state champion Eastern Cottonwood is 80 feet tall and has a crown spread of 100 feet and a trunk circumference of 372 inches. It is growing in Bandera County.

PLAINS COTTONWOOD. *Populus sargentii.*

Plains Cottonwood is considered by some to be a variety of Eastern Cottonwood, but it differs by having about half as many teeth on each side of the leaf blade and bud scales slightly hairy rather than smooth. It is common along streams and rivers, ponds, and roadside ditches throughout the Plains regions of North Central Texas and the Panhandle areas. In some parts of its range it is the only plant reaching tree size.

RIO GRANDE COTTONWOOD

Populus wislizenii.
Large deciduous tree to about 100 feet tall with a broad open crown and short stout trunk to 3 feet or more in diameter.

Leaves — Alternate, on slender leaf stalks 1½ to 3 inches wide and 1½ to 3 inches in length, thick and firm, light yellowish green.

Flowers — In spring or early summer, the sexes on separate trees. Male catkins 1½ to 2 inches long, densely flowered; female flowers slender about 4½ inches in length.

Fruit—Capsules narrowly egg-shaped about ¼ inch long, with light brown seeds covered with silky hairs.

Twigs — Stout, light green at first turning yellow gray, terminal winter buds about ¼ inch long pointed at the tip, laterals about half as long.

Bark — Light gray or brownish, smooth when young but becoming thick and splitting longitudinally, turning rough later.

Rio Grande Cottonwood is probably the most common *Populus* species seen along waterways and ponds throughout West Texas. The weak wood is light, soft, and somewhat brownish. It is used mostly for fuel and fence posts but poles made from the trunks were used for adobe house frames and rafters. This tree is fast growing and relatively short-lived and has some value as a shade tree.

Indian women used strips of inner bark in their clothing and wove baskets from the young twigs. The catkins can be eaten raw and the inner bark was chewed as a food supplement to prevent scurvy. Rio Grande Cottonwood is a favorite nesting place for many species of birds, and the twigs and leaves are browsed by mule deer and cattle. Horses and cattle also gnaw at the inner bark. The national champion Rio Grande Cottonwood is located in Jeff Davis County and is 342 inches in circumference, 110 feet tall, and has a crown spread of 127 feet.

NARROW LEAF COTTONWOOD. *Populus angustifolia.*

A small to medium sized tree about 40 feet or more tall with a narrow, somewhat conical, crown and a slender trunk 18 inches in diameter. It is an uncommon tree found along streams in the Trans-Pecos mountains and can be distinguished from other *Populus* sp. by its leaves which are about 3 times longer than broad. Western Indians used the young

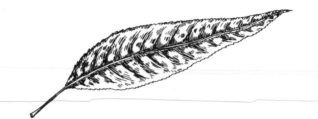

branchlets for basket making and collected a honey-like residue from the leaf undersides which is exuded by aphids and employed it as a substitute for sugar.

QUAKING ASPEN. *Populus tremuloides.*

Differs from Rio Grande Cottonwood by having leaves more rounded or egg-shaped and fine teeth on the margins rather than being coarsely toothed. It is found at elevations above 7,000 feet in ravines and on slopes in the Trans-Pecos mountains. This is the most widely distributed tree in North America but in Texas its range is limited to the Guadalupe Mountains, the north slopes of the Chisos Mountains, and on Mount Livermore in the Davis Mountains.

AMERICAN HOP HORNBEAM

Ostrya virginiana.
Eastern Hop Hornbeam, Ironwood.
A small deciduous tree about 30 feet
tall with a trunk 10 inches or so in diameter. Under forest conditions it develops a slender, straight, unbranched trunk with an
open crown of gracefully drooping thin branches. In the
open the trunk is short with a broad crown.

Leaves — Alternate, simple, 2 to 4 inches in length, firm and
somewhat translucent, downy hairy on both surfaces,
dull yellow green above, paler beneath. Turning yellow
in the fall.
Flowers — Sexes separate but on the same tree, appearing in
spring with developing leaves. Male catkins are in small

clusters of up to three and are formed in the fall. They persist over the winter as scaly cylindrical buds less than ½ inch long located at the branch tips. In the spring, they open and grow to about 2 inches long. Female catkins are found at the ends of new growth from the current year.

Fruit — Maturing in late summer to early fall. The small flat nutlets are borne in 2-inch-long drooping clusters of bladdery sacs that look like hops.

Twigs — Slender, without a true terminal bud, giving them a slightly zigzag appearance, somewhat hairy, yellow orange to brown.

Bark — Very distinctive, smooth and tight. Thin, gray or brown, on older trunks turning into shreddy vertical strips, turned out at the tips.

American Hop Hornbeam is usually found as an understory tree in moist forests or fairly dry hills in the Piney Woods area of East Texas. The wood of American Hop Hornbeam has a thick white sapwood and a reddish-brown heartwood and is extremely hard and tough, hence the common name "Ironwood." It is usually a small tree and no longer of much commercial importance, but it was formerly used for tool handles, fuel, sled runners, wagon-wheel rims, spokes, and axles. The Indians sometimes used the wood for bows.

Ironwood is a graceful, small tree with no serious pests or disease problems. It tolerates shade, but it is slow growing and the thin bark is easily damaged. If the tree is pruned in the spring when the sap is beginning to run it will bleed profusely. The winter flower and leaf buds, as well as the seeds, are eaten by a variety of birds. The state champion American Hop Hornbeam is in the Sabine National Forest. It is 34 inches in circumference, 62 feet tall, and has a crown spread of 36 feet.

WESTERN HOP HORNBEAM. *Ostrya knowltonii.*

A small tree to about 25 feet tall that is a western version of American Hop Hornbeam. In Texas, it is restricted to the Trans-Pecos area and can be found scattered in canyons of the Guadalupe Mountains National Park.

BIG BEND HOP HORNBEAM. *Ostrya chisosensis.*

Differs from Western Hop Hornbeam by not having stalked glands on the leaves and being restricted to the Chisos Mountains of the Big Bend National Park. The national champion Big Bend Hop Hornbeam is 32 feet tall, 28 inches in circumference, and shades an area 24 feet across.

AMERICAN HORNBEAM

Carpinus caroliniana.
Ironwood, Blue Beech.
A small attractive deciduous tree to 30 feet tall with a rounded bushy crown and a crooked, often flattened or fluted, trunk to one foot in diameter.

Leaves — Alternate, simple, deciduous, 2-3 inches long, young leaves hairy, older ones blue green and smooth above, light yellowish and relatively smooth below, turning red or pink in the fall before dropping.

Flowers — In the spring, sexes separate but on the same tree. Male flowers in thin, drooping clusters, catkins about 1 inch in length, females in small catkins about ½ inch long at the branch tips.

Fruit — Maturing in late summer to fall as hanging clusters, up to 5 inches in length, of stiff three-lobed bracts about 2 inches long that look like leaves, each with a small ribbed nutlet at the base. Often persisting after the leaves have fallen.

68

Twigs — Slender, tough, slightly zigzagged, light green and hairy when young, turning pale gray and smooth when older, occasionally drooping at the tips.
Bark — Blue gray, thin, tight and smooth.

American Hornbeam is a shade-tolerant understory tree found in moist woods, river bottoms, and near streams throughout the East Texas pine forests. It is readily recognized by the twisted trunk which is vertically fluted on older trees. Even though it likes moisture, American Hornbeam cannot tolerate flooding. The wood is white with a small, brownish-white heartwood. It is very heavy, hard, close grained, and not usually subject to splitting or cracking, making it an ideal wood for bowls, dishes, and handles for striking tools such as hammers, but the small size and crooked form make it difficult to obtain usable wood.

As an ornamental, American Hornbeam is slow-growing, short-lived, and the thin bark is easily damaged; however, it has no serious pests or diseases, nice fall color most years, and a distinctive picturesque appearance. The tree is only of slight importance to wildlife. The state champion American Hornbeam is 49 feet tall and has a trunk circumference of 60 inches and a crown spread of 46 feet. It is owned by the Texas Department of Highways and Public Transportation and is found in Newton County.

RIVER BIRCH

Betula nigra.
Graceful, medium sized deciduous tree to 90 feet tall with a broad spreading crown and a short trunk about 2 feet thick that divides early.

Leaves — Alternate, simple, 1 to 3 inches long, thick and tough in texture. Dark green and shiny on top, paler and, when young, somewhat downy below. Turning bright yellow before dropping in the fall.

70

Flowers — In early spring, male and female flowers on the same tree but in separate catkins. Male catkins drooping, shiny dark brown, 2 to 3 inches in length; female catkins bright green upright, about ¼ inch long.

Fruit — Ripening late spring – early summer, hanging cylinder-shaped cones about 1 inch long with each scale covering a single small winged seed.

Twigs — Slender, dark red, smooth and shiny, developing a thin peeling bark by the third year. The reddish cast of the twigs from a distance makes winter identification easy from the road.

Bark — Thin, light reddish brown, peeling to expose the salmon pink bark underneath when young, becoming thicker and silvery gray with shaggy papery strips on old trees.

River Birch is found in moist soil along rivers, streams, creeks, ponds, and the edges of swamps of the pine forests of East Texas. River Birch wood is light and strong, close grained, and light brown in color but is seldom used commercially. This is an attractive ornamental tree because of the peeling bark, graceful form, fast growth rate, and reasonably good fall color. However, it is relatively short-lived, does poorly on heavy dry soils, and even though it likes being near water it does not tolerate flooding very well. The tiny seeds are produced in great abundance and are a good wildlife food. Besides being an attractive ornamental it is also good for erosion control along stream and river banks. River Birch is the only birch species native to Texas and is the only birch species to have fruits that mature in late spring.

71

SMOOTH ALDER

Alnus serrulata.
Hazel Alder.
Small deciduous tree to about 15 feet
tall or a large spreading shrub.

Leaves — Alternate, simple, 2-5 inches in length, somewhat
thick, dark green and smooth on top, brownish green and
usually hairy beneath.

Flowers — Very early in the spring, sexes separate but on the
same tree. The male catkins 2-5 clustered at the branch

tips, drooping, about 3 inches long; female catkins about ¼ inch long at the ends of the branches, usually somewhat purplish.

Fruit — Little cones about ¾ inch long ripening late summer–early fall but persisting over the winter.

Twigs — Slender, lacking a true terminal bud, which gives them a somewhat zigzag appearance. The male cones for the following year are often found as clustered cylindrical buds at the branch tips. Lateral buds are on short stalks.

Bark — Thin and tight, smooth and gray with prominent lenticels.

Smooth Alder is frequently found close to water, at the edge of streams, lakes, and swamps in East Texas west to about Leon County. It is a relatively short-lived tree that grows quickly and will not tolerate shade. This might be a desirable ornamental for wet areas because of the fast growth, nice gray bark, and in early spring the hanging male catkins are prominently displayed. The thin bark of Smooth Alder, however, is easily damaged and the growth form can be scraggly and unsymmetrical. The bark contains tannic acid and was once used medicinally as an astringent and to treat fevers. The little cones are often sold in flea markets and novelty stores as "Baby Pine Cones" and used as decor on Christmas wreaths. The state champion Smooth Alder is 37 feet tall and has a crown spread of 24 feet and a trunk circumference of 14 inches. It is growing in Jasper County.

AMERICAN BEECH

Fagus grandifolia.
Beechnut.
A beautiful large deciduous tree over 100 feet tall and 3 feet in diameter. Either a slender tree with a long straight trunk in the forest or with a short thick trunk and a broad spreading crown in the open.

Leaves — Alternate, simple, 3 to 6 inches long. Dark green and shiny above, lighter and yellow green below. The veins are prominent and run straight to the edge of the leaf. The leaves usually turn yellow in the fall, then turn brown and often remain on the tree through the winter.

Flowers — In early spring with the new leaves, both sexes on the same tree. The male flowers are in round, fluffy, stalked heads about 1 inch across, and the female flowers are in clusters of two's at the base of the upper leaves.
Fruit — Maturing in the fall. The brown-shelled, three-angled nuts are about ¾ inch long with a sweet edible meat and are enclosed in a bur covered with relatively flimsy spines.
Twigs — Slender, slightly zigzagged with long pointed buds up to 1 inch in length.
Bark — Very distinctive, thin and tight, light gray, often bearing the carvings of passersby — initials, dates, hearts, etc.

American Beech is usually found in rich, moist woods and along streams in deep East Texas west to about the Trinity River. Beech wood is straight grained, hard, heavy with a whitish sapwood and a light red heartwood; it looks a lot like oak but is more even grained. The wood has many commercial uses such as charcoal, railroad ties, boxes and crates, handles and brush backs, pallets, curved portions of furniture, violin backs, and fuelwood.

Beech is a handsome tree in cultivation, casts a dense shade, tolerates shade itself, and is reasonably free of serious pests and diseases. On the other hand, the roots are fairly shallow and many plants (such as lawn grass) will hardly grow under the heavy shade they produce; the thin bark is easily damaged and often disfigured by sentimental carvings. The tasty nuts are eagerly eaten by many species of wildlife from birds to foxes. The state champion Beech is located in the Sabine National Forest. It is 150 inches in circumference, 132 feet tall, and has a crown spread of 66 feet.

75

ALLEGHENY CHINQUAPIN

Castanea pumila.
Chinquapin.
A large deciduous tree about 30 feet tall with a broad, rounded crown. Usually branching near the base into several trunks up to 1 foot in diameter.

Leaves — Alternate, simple, 2½ to 6 inches long, firm, shiny bright green above with a white hairy underside.

Flowers — In spring to early summer, the 5-inch-long yellowish-white male catkins are in somewhat showy clusters at the end of the new branches. The female flowers are scattered at the base of the male catkins.

Fruit — Maturing in the fall as spiny burs about 1½ inches across, enclosing a tasty nut to 1 inch in length.

Twigs — Slender, light reddish brown, hairy when young, becoming smooth and dark brown later. Buds rusty red, hairy.

Bark — Light reddish brown with distinctive, often silver or gray, flat ridges and shallow furrows, fairly thick.

Chinquapins are commonly found in dryish, upland, sandy soils in the East Texas Piney Woods. The hard wood is attractive with a whitish sapwood and brown heartwood but is seldom used commercially because of the tree's small size and tendency to branch into several trunks low to the ground. These trees have ornamental possibilities due to their shiny green leaves, showy flower tassels, good growth rate, and drought resistance. They are not without drawbacks, however, as the trunks often branch low to the ground and the spiny burs make going barefoot hazardous. The seeds are sweet but difficult and often painful to extract from the needle-sharp spiny burs. After the kernels are removed from the burs they can be roasted and coated with sugar to make a type of candy.

This is our closest relative to the once great American Chestnut (*Castanea dentata*) that has been virtually wiped out by the chestnut blight. The name Chinquapin comes from an Indian term for chestnut. There are several varieties of Chinquapins that form a complex based on leaf hairs and plant size.

THE OAKS

The oaks can be divided into three fairly distinct groups — Red Oaks, White Oaks, and the Live Oaks. (The Live Oaks are sometimes split into a fourth category, the Willow Oaks.) Each major category has characteristic features that help in field identification throughout the seasons. It does help to use mature foliage because juvenile oak leaves are highly variable and often bear no resemblance to the adult forms.

RED OAKS HAVE THE FOLLOWING
CHARACTERISTICS:
1. Sharply-lobed leaves with relatively soft tiny spines (aristae) on their tips.

2. Acorns that take two years to mature. They spend the first year as little scaly buds on the twigs. The mature fruits are generally high in tannic acid.
3. Winter buds that are usually sharply pointed at the tips.
4. Black or dark gray bark roughened into ridges or blocks.
5. Water-conducting vessels clear of obstructing cells (see below for details).

WHITE OAKS HAVE THE FOLLOWING
CHARACTERISTICS:
1. Leaves that have rounded lobes or teeth and are
   not armed with a spine tip (marginal aristae).

2. Acorns that mature the same year (annually) and
   are usually fairly low in tannic acid content.
3. Winter buds that are mostly rounded at the tip.
4. Light gray scaly bark with gray ridges and furrows
   on older specimens.
5. Water-conducting vessels plugged up by a peculiar
   phenomenon called tylosis. This is where cells adjacent to the vessels swell out and obstruct the pas-
   sage. When the wood is dried and cut, these cells
   appear somewhat shiny. These tylosis cells give the
   white oak wood relative impermeability (tight
   cooperage), enabling it to be used for water storage,
   whiskey barrels, and to better withstand certain
   vascular diseases.

THE LIVE OAKS:
   Share some characteristics of both other groups
   and are mainly distinguished by their usually evergreen, somewhat elliptical, leaves. The fourth
   group, the Willow Oaks, is sometimes separated
   from the Live Oaks but for this treatment will be
   absorbed into the Live Oak category.

CHISOS RED OAK

Quercus gravesii.
Graves Oak.
A red oak growing up to 40 feet tall,
with dark, roughly furrowed bark.

Leaves — Deciduous, 2-5 inches long, dark green and shiny
above, pale underneath, occasionally with hairs. Two or
three deep lobes on each side ending in a bristle-like tip.
Flowers — Male catkin 4 inches long, hairy; female flowers
minute, 1-3 flowered.

80

Fruit — Acorn ½ inch long, light brown, top-shaped, rounded at the tip. One third to ½ enclosed in a saucer-shaped cup. Maturing the second year.
Twigs — Slender, reddish brown.
Bark — Dark gray to black, deeply furrowed.

Chisos Red Oak is found growing in the high canyon areas of the Trans-Pecos region of Texas and Coahuila, Mexico. This oak, known for its brilliant show of red and yellow fall colors, is most abundant in the Chisos Mountains. It is generally found above 5,000 feet on the moist, north-facing slopes or shaded canyon areas. Chisos Oak is usually associated with other woodland species such as Pinyon Pine, Alligator Juniper, Bigtooth Maple, Emory and Gray Oak. The leaves are often browsed by deer and the acorns ripening in September are consumed by turkeys, quail, and ground squirrels. The acorns are also edible by humans and were often ground into flour by the Indians. Chisos Red Oak is closely related to Texas or Spanish Oak *Quercus texana,* and to Chisos Oak *Q. graciliformis*—a small tree from the Chisos Mts. with long narrow, slightly lobed or toothed leaves.

81

Fagaceae - Beech Family

TEXAS OAK

Quercus buckleyi. [*Quercus texana*].
Texas Red Oak, Spanish Oak.
A small to medium sized deciduous tree up to 40 feet, often multi-trunked.

Leaves — 2½ to 5 inches long, 2 to 3½ inches wide, 3- to 7-lobed, dark green and shiny above, paler below.

Flowers — Male and female catkins on the same tree. Male catkins hairy, 1 to 3½ inches long, female catkins 1½ to 3½ inches long, 1-3 flowered, stigmas red.

Fruit — Acorn oval-shaped, ½ to ¾ inch long, reddish brown, pubescent, often striped with dark lines, ¼ to ½ enclosed in cup, borne singly or paired.

Twigs — Reddish brown when young, turning gray later.
Bark — Brown to gray with platelike scales, deeply fissured,
sometimes smooth and gray.

The Texas or Spanish Oak grows on limestone hills and ridges in North Central and Central Texas on the Edwards Plateau west to the Pecos River. This tree is often growing in association with Ashe Juniper, Live Oak, Lacey Oak, Texas Ash, or Black Cherry. During the fall, the Texas Red Oak provides quite a show, dotting the hillsides with bright shades of scarlet and orange. It is found predominantly on north and east exposures where soils are somewhat cooler and moister. The Texas Red Oak wood is used locally for fence posts and fuel.

Many species of wildlife such as scrub jays, turkey, squirrels, and whitetail deer eat the abundant acorns. The rare golden-cheeked warbler which nests in the Hill Country is dependent upon not only the Ashe Juniper but also the Texas Oak for its nesting success. The bird collects strips of mature juniper bark for nest material and then binds it together with webbing from the tent caterpillars found on the Texas Red Oak. The caterpillars from these webs are later fed to the newly-hatched chicks. The Texas Red Oak is a popular landscape tree because of its moderate to fast growth, good form, and reliable fall color. Care should be taken, however, if buying a tree collected from the wild as they often develop a fatal fungal canker (*Hypoxylon* sp.) on the trunk. Some botanists feel that Texas Oak is merely a variety of the Shumard Oak found growing in drier, limestone soils.

Fagaceae - Beech Family

BLACKJACK OAK

Quercus marilandica.
Small deciduous tree about 30 feet tall with a rounded crown, often with pendant lower branches. The short trunk grows to about 1 foot in diameter.

Leaves — Alternate, leathery, 3 to 7 inches long, 2 to 5 inches wide across the broadest part. Shiny and dark green above, brown and hairy beneath, turning dull red in fall and often hanging on the tree throughout much of the winter.

Flowers — In spring with the new leaves, male catkins slender 4 to 5 inches in length, female catkins about ¼ inch long at the end of the twigs.

Fruit — Acorns maturing the second year, ripening late fall to early winter. About ¾ inch long with the cup enclosing half of the nut.

Twigs — Stout and stiff. Brown and hairy at first, becoming gray later; the winter buds red hairy, sharp pointed, and often over ¼ inch long.

Bark — Dark, almost black, and broken into rough blocky plates.

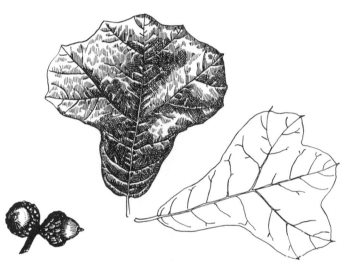

Blackjack Oak is said to usually indicate poor sites as it is often found on dry sandy or gravelly soils throughout East and Central Texas west to about Callahan County. Combined with Post Oak and Texas Hickory, this tree is associated with one of the most characteristic woodland regions of Texas. The wood has many of the desirable qualities of Red Oak but is usually so small it is only used for firewood and fence posts. It is rarely cultivated because of its relatively slow growth and because it is difficult to transplant. The acorns are eaten by wild turkey and white-tailed deer; they are rich in tannins and require extensive leaching to become edible for humans.

Fagaceae - Beech Family

SHUMARD OAK

Quercus shumardii.
Red Oak.
A large tree 100 feet or more tall with an open, spreading crown and a long symmetrical trunk 2 to 3 feet in diameter.

Leaves — Alternate, simple, deciduous, 5 to 8 inches long, dark green, smooth and shiny on top, paler beneath, turning red in the fall.

Flowers — In spring, male catkins 5 to 7 inches in length, females in short spikes ½ inch long.
Fruit — Maturing in the fall of the second year, singly or in pairs, nut about 1 inch long, resting in a thick shallow cup covering about ½ of the length of the acorns.
Twigs — Slender to thickish, smooth, gray to reddish brown, terminal buds pointed about ¼ inch long.
Bark — Light brown to gray or black, smooth at first but developing into tight furrows or plates.

Shumard Oak is usually found scattered in moist woods and along streams in the eastern third of Texas. It is considered one of the largest and fastest growing of the southern red oaks in Texas. This is a good shade tree for lawns or parklands within its range and where moisture is adequate outside its range. They transplant well and have beautiful fall color. Healthy trees have few problems but stressed individuals are susceptible to some insect and disease problems. On dry sites, this oak grows slowly and will often turn chlorotic. The acorns are eaten by various species of wildlife such as deer, squirrels, and turkeys. Shumard Oak was named for Benjamin F. Shumard, an early state geologist of Texas. Our state champion Shumard Oak is 182 inches in circumference, 120 feet tall, and has a crown spread of 92 feet. It is located in the Alabama-Coushatta Indian Reservation near Livingston.

NUTTALL OAK. *Quercus nuttallii.*

An uncommon tree of deep river bottoms that differs from Shumard Oak by having a deeper acorn cup and more deeply lobed leaves.

SOUTHERN RED OAK

Quercus falcata.
Spanish Oak.
Large tree to 70 feet or more tall with
an open round-topped crown made of
stout branches and a straight trunk
2-3 feet in diameter.

Leaves — Alternate, simple, deciduous, 3-9 inches long, dark
green and shiny on top, covered with brown or gray fuzz
below, turning orange or red brown before dropping in
the fall. Usually with 5 to 7 deep lobes but some plants
show only 3 stumpy ones. The typically somewhat-
rounded leaf bases help distinguish this species from
other East Texas red oaks.

Flowers — Appearing in the spring as the leaves begin to unfold, the sexes on the same tree as hairy catkins 3-5 inches long, and female flowers single or up to three in small clusters borne on a short, thick, downy stalk.

Fruit — Rounded acorns with thin shallow cups ripening in early fall of the second year, up to ½ inch long, orange brown, usually hairy, borne singly or in pairs on short stalks.

Twigs — Fairly stout, covered with light brown or gray hair at first, becoming smooth with age. Buds red, hairy, scaly, and pointed.

Bark — Smooth and gray at first, soon turning rough and darker, eventually becoming almost black.

Southern Red Oak is probably the most common red oak species in the forests of East Texas west and south to Lamar, Brazos, and Brazoria counties. It is mainly an upland species but is not generally found on very dry sites. This species occupies a transitional role in forest succession from pioneer to climax cover. The wood is rather typical of Red Oak being light red with a lighter sapwood, heavy, hard, strong, and close grained. It is used mostly for boxes, crates, pallets, furniture, flooring, and is a good firewood selection. In rural East Texas almost every old country church has an older Southern Red Oak growing nearby. Dirt roads often part and rejoin to make room for growing specimens. This oak used to be a favorite shade tree because of its fast growth and longevity, but is not often planted today.

Q. falcata is sometimes mistaken by unknowing land-scape architects as Spanish Oak/Texas Red Oak (*Quercus texana*) and planted on the clay soils of Central Texas where they languish and die. Stressed trees are prone to problems such as borers, and the relatively thin bark is readily injured by fire and mowers. The acorns are usually borne in abundance and are relied upon by many species of wildlife including deer, turkeys, songbirds, and squirrels who are largely responsible for the seed dispersal. The state champion Southern Red Oak is located in the Sabine National Forest, Sabine County. It is 128 feet tall, has a trunk circumference of 193 inches, and shades an area 97 feet across.

CHERRY BARK OAK. *Quercus pagodaefolia* or *Quercus falcata* var. *pagodaefolia*.
Swamp Spanish Oak.

A large tree to 80 feet or more found in moist areas throughout the East Texas Piney Woods. The distinctive "pagoda" leaf shape, gray scaly bark, and robust nature readily distinguish this from other East Texas red oaks. Cherry Bark Oak produces superior red oak lumber and is an important wildlife food, particularly for ducks, squirrels, deer, and turkeys. This would be an outstanding shade or park tree on moist sites within its natural range, but stressed trees are subject to borers and the relatively thin bark is easily damaged.

91

BLACK OAK

Quercus velutina.
Medium sized tree about 70 feet tall with a rounded crown and a trunk 2 to 3 feet in diameter.

Leaves — Alternate, simple, deciduous, about seven inches long, crimson red when first unfolding in the spring, later becoming dark green and shiny above and yellow-green and somewhat brown hairy beneath when mature.

Flowers — Developing in spring when the leaves are half grown, the male flowers are in catkins about 5 inches long and the female flowers are barely noticeable on short spikes.

Fruit — Maturing in the fall of the second year, borne singly or in pairs, ½ to ¾ inch long, the acorn cup length is variable, and the inside of the cup has a yellow lining. Acorn kernel is yellow and is very bitter due to the high tannic acid content.

Twigs — Slender to moderately stout, reddish brown at first and somewhat hairy but becoming smooth with age. Terminal buds reddish brown to brown and rather squared, about ¼ to ½ inch long.

Bark — Dark brown and smooth at first but developing into rough black thick ridges and deep fissures. The inner bark is sometimes bright yellow or orange.

Black Oak is generally found on well-drained upland sites throughout the Piney Woods of East Texas venturing westward to Waller and Anderson counties. The wood of Black Oak is considered inferior to other Red Oak species because it is generally defective and does not cure well. It is a somewhat short-lived tree and does not have a particularly handsome growth form but has ornamental value in its ability to thrive on poor sites unsuited to better species. The bark contains a high amount of tannin and was formerly used for preparing a yellow dye for coloring wool and silk and for tanning skins. A drug, scarcely available today, was formerly obtained from the bark for medicinal purposes as a mild astringent. The bitter acorns are eaten by a number of wildlife species including deer, turkeys, and squirrels.

GAMBEL OAK

Quercus gambelii.
Shrub or small tree with a rounded crown, usually growing 15 to 30 feet tall.

Leaves — Deciduous, 2½ to 7 inches long, deeply divided lobes, dark green above, with pale green, often fuzzy undersides.
Flowers — Male catkins brown, hairy 1½ inch long; female flowers minute in the junctions of the branchlets.

94

Fruit— Acorn ½ to ¾ inch long; ⅓ to ½ enclosed in a bowl-like cup with hairy scales; matures in one season.
Twigs — Stout, reddish brown at first, becoming darker with age.
Bark — Gray to brown, becoming rough and scaly with age.

Gambel Oak is the most common deciduous oak of the Southern Rocky Mountains. In Texas, this oak occurs only at highter altitudes in the Guadalupe, Chisos, and Davis mountains (usually above 6,000 feet). It often forms thickets covering hillsides, particularly after a disturbance of some kind, and is a very slow growing oak. Gambel Oak wood is heavy and durable, but because of its poor form and its inaccessibility, the wood is of little commercial value. Locally, it may be used for fuel, fencing, farm tools, and mine timbers. Gambel Oak leaves are browsed by horses, cows, deer, and porcupines. Turkeys, jays, javelina, and squirrels eat the acorns. Like the fruit of the Emory Oak, these sweet acorns were ground into a flour by the Indians.

HAVARD SHIN OAK

Quercus havardii.
Shin Oak.
A deciduous shrub to about 3 feet tall forming extensive thickets, or a small gnarly tree up to 25 feet tall.

Leaves — Deciduous ¾ to 4 inches long, variable in shape, shiny, smooth above but often somewhat hairy beneath.

Flowers — In mid spring as the leaves unfold as separate sexed catkins; males about 1 inch long, females in short spikes less than ½ inch long.

Fruit — Maturing in early fall of the first year, ½ to 1 inch in diameter, borne singly or in clusters of up to 3.

Twigs — Slender, rounded or somewhat ribbed in cross section, densely yellow hairy when young, becoming gray to reddish brown and smooth with age.

Bark — Thin gray and smooth, then becoming scaly at maturity.

Havard Shin Oak is found on deep sandy soils in the lower Texas Panhandle area west into eastern New Mexico. It has spread out over vast areas forming one of the shortest but most extensive oak forests in North America. In the deep sands where this plant grows, the aboveground part seldom reaches over three feet tall but the underground root systems can reach depths of 90 feet. These wide-spreading roots serve an important role in erosion control, stabilizing acres and acres of shifting sands. The large acorns are eaten by deer, javelina, quail, and prairie chickens. The national champion Havard Shin Oak can be found in Yoakum County. It is 30 feet tall, has a trunk girth of 40 inches, and covers an area of 23 feet.

97

WHITE SHIN OAK

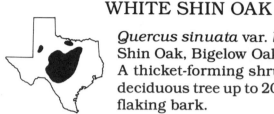

Quercus sinuata var. *breviloba*.
Shin Oak, Bigelow Oak.
A thicket-forming shrub or a small
deciduous tree up to 20 feet tall with
flaking bark.

Leaves — Alternate, 1½ to 4 inches long, quite variable in shape,
grayish green, lower surface paler, sometimes pubescent,
upper surface often with minute star-shaped tufts of
hairs.

Flowers — Male catkins 1-2 inches long, pubescent, anthers red;
female catkin shorter, also pubescent, 1 to 3 flowered.

Fruit — Acorns borne singly or paired, ½ to 1 inch long, yellowish brown to brown.

Twigs — Gray to brown, often pubescent.

Bark — Gray, thin, and flaking.

White Shin Oak is found predominantly on limestone hills of Central Texas, West Texas, Mexico, and into southern Oklahoma. On the western edge of its range it forms low-growing shrubby thickets, while on the eastern end in deeper soils, small, single-trunked, crooked trees are found. This Oak is sometimes confused with Lacey Oak on the Edwards Plateau as the leaves are very similar. Shin Oak has shaggy or flaking bark, however, while Lacey does not. Shin Oak also usually has minute tufts of star-shaped hairs on the upper leaf surface. The national champion White Shin Oak is in Austin and stands 39 feet tall with a crown spread of 34 feet.

DURAND OAK. *Quercus durandii.*

A medium sized tree about 50 feet tall with a trunk two feet in diameter. It differs from White Shin Oak by being a larger, solitary tree associated with river bottoms in East and Central Texas. This is one of the dominant trees in Palmetto State Park but is relatively uncommon throughout its range. Some large specimens can also be found on the University of Texas campus in Austin. This tree and Nutmeg Hickory (*Carya myristicaeformis*) are considered by

some authorities to be relics of an earlier floral age because they have similar spotty distributions. The state champion Durand Oak belongs to the City of Waco Parks and Recreation Department in McLennan County. It is 81 feet tall, has a trunk girth of 97 inches, and shades an area 57 feet across.

LACEY OAK

Quercus laceyi.
[*Quercus glaucoides*]. Blue Oak.
A small to medium sized deciduous
tree to 45 feet with a blue-gray cast.

Leaves — Leathery, 2-5 inches long, lobed, upper surface blue gray or grayish green, lower surface paler, sometimes with hairs along the veins, often turning yellow to pinkish in the fall.

Flowers — In the spring, in separate male and female catkins.

Fruit — Acorns, brown, oval, enclosed in a cup ¼ to ½ its length, borne singly or in a cluster of 2 or 3.

Twigs — Fuzzy, light brown turning gray and glabrous later.

Bark — Gray to dark brown, broken into narrow longitudinal fissures, later forming small square plates.

101

Lacey Oak is a shrubby small to medium sized tree found growing only on rocky limestone hills, ravines, and canyons of the Edwards Plateau in Texas and in mountains of Mexico south to Oaxaca. The blue-gray foliage seen from a distance gives it a smokey appearance, due in part to a very thin waxlike surface on the leaves that serves to inhibit moisture loss. Lacey Oak can easily be confused with White Shin Oak on upland sites but the latter has shaggy or flaking bark and leaves with some minute starlike hairs on the surface.

The Lacey Oak is named for Howard Lacey who discovered the tree on his ranch near Kerrville. Some people in the Hill Country call this tree "Blue Oak."

The wood has been used for fuel and posts. Lacey Oak is gaining popularity as a landscape tree for the Central Texas area because it is drought resistant and the attractive bluish leaves occasionally display late fall color. Like other members of the white oak group, it is less susceptible to the oak wilt fungus which is devastating areas of the Hill Country. The national champion Lacey Oak is found in Blanco County. It stands 58 feet tall, has a crown spread of 96 feet and a trunk circumference of 107 inches.

CHINKAPIN OAK

Quercus muhlenbergii.
Chinquapin Oak.
A deciduous oak up to 50 feet tall with a straight trunk and a spreading crown.

Leaves — Oblong, pointed at the tip, toothed or notched on the edges, 4-6 inches long, 1-4 inches wide, upper surface shiny dark green, paler and slightly fuzzy on the underside.

103

Flowers — Male and female on the same tree in separate catkins, males light yellow hairy, 3-4 inches long; female flowers minute, 1 to 5 on a short stalk at the base of the leaf.

Fruit — Acorn oval-shaped, ½ to 1¼ inches long, about ½ enclosed in cup, brown to black. Acorn maturing in one year.

Twigs — Slightly fuzzy when young, becoming smooth and reddish brown with age, terminal buds orange to reddish brown.

Bark — Light gray, breaking into narrow plates.

The Chinkapin Oak is found in limestone soils at the base of bluffs and protected canyon areas of East, Central, North Central, and West Texas. It is often growing near streams associated with Black Cherry and Walnut, and at Lost Maples State Natural Area it is quite abundant alongside the Bigtooth Maples. The attractive saw-toothed leaves are quite distinctive, similar in appearance to the true Chinquapin (*Castanea pumila*) of the eastern United States, hence the common name. In the fall, the leaves of Chinkapin Oak often turn a slight bronze color; the tree is moderate to fast growing. Although in Texas, Chinkapin Oaks rarely grow over 50 to 60 feet tall, in the midwest and eastern United States, trees 100 feet tall can be seen.

The wood of this tree is heavy and durable. It has been used for split-rail fences, panels, railroad ties, and fuel, but is of little commercial value today because of its relative scarcity. The acorns are sweet and readily eaten by turkeys, quail, deer, raccoons, and squirrels. A palatable flour can be made from these acorn after boiling the tannins off. The attractive leaf, handsome form, and moderate-to-fast growth make the Chinkapin a good shade tree for many areas of Texas. The state champion Chinkapin Oak is found in Newton County; it stands 86 feet tall, has a trunk circumference of 171 inches, and shades an area 86 feet across.

SWAMP CHESTNUT OAK. *Quercus prinus* or *Quercus michauxii.*
Basket Oak.

A large tree to 80 feet tall or more, found in moist woods associated with major streams and rivers in East Texas from Marion to Brazoria counties. It can be distinguished from Chinkapin Oak by its woolly leaf undersurfaces, deeper toothed margins, the acorn cup enclosing the nut for about a third of its length, and a preference for bottomland habitats. The wood is rather typical of the white oak group: heavy, strong, hard, and durable, with the ability to split along the growth rings making excellent splints for baskets and barrel staves. Unlike other oaks, the acorns have a relatively low tannic acid content and require little leaching to be edible for humans. On moist sites, this oak has good potential as a shade tree because of its longevity and few pest or disease problems.

105

Fagaceae - Beech Family

POST OAK

Quercus stellata.
Medium to large tree 50 feet or more in height with a broad rounded crown and a thick, sometimes leaning, trunk 2 feet in diameter.

Leaves — Alternate, deciduous, the brown leaves often persisting on the branches through the winter, 4-5 inches in length with variable lobing, the most characteristic being two strong arms forming a distinctive cross shape. The upper surface is dark green and shiny while the lower surface is lighter and covered with minute, star-shaped hairs visible with a hand lens.

Flowers — Appearing in the spring when the leaves are about one-third unfolded, the male catkins are up to 5 inches in length while the minute female flowers are borne in inconspicuous clusters.

Fruit — Ripening in early fall, maturing in one season, as ovoid acorns up to 1 inch long with a relatively small cup.

Twigs — Stout and gray-brown hairy with rounded buds.

Bark — Somewhat thin and gray-brown scaly at first, becoming thick and fairly distinctive, developing deep longitudinal fissures separating rounded, dark gray ridges.

Post Oak is one of the most widespread oaks in Texas. It covers the eastern two-thirds of the state north to Wheeler County, west to Howard and Edwards counties, and south to Goliad County. In most areas it is usually found on scattered dry upland situations, but in East Texas it ranges down into moist areas. This tree is dominant in the sandy areas of North and East Central Texas where it forms the vegetational region known as the "Post Oak Savannah." Some of its frequent companions are Blackjack Oak and Texas Hickory.

The wood of Post Oak is similar to other members of the white oak group: hard, heavy, and resistant to decay when in contact with the ground. Post Oak usually has a gnarly growth habit which offers little in merchantable timber except for fence posts or railroad ties (which it was used for extensively before the days of creosote). The Post Oaks are

107

rugged shade trees, suitable for otherwise inhospitable locations. With the persistent dead branches removed they become handsome specimens that have few pest problems, endure drought, and the thick bark resists fire damage and lawn equipment. Many species of wildlife eat the acorns, and the tree provides much-needed cover in upland areas. The wide variation in leaf shape and site preference has given rise to several species considered only varieties by some authorities. Two of the best accepted species/varieties are:

SWAMP POST OAK. *Quercus similis* or *Q. stellata* var. *similis.*

Distinguished from other Post Oaks by having leaves with narrow lobes that are seldom arranged in a cross-shaped pattern and ranging along river and stream bottoms in East and Southeast Texas.

SAND POST OAK. *Quercus margaretta* or *Q. stellata* var. *margaretta.*
Runner Oak.

A scrubby, small tree or suckering shrub having thin leaves rounded on the lobe tips and found growing on sandy soils in East and Central Texas.

BUR OAK

Quercus macrocarpa.
Mossy Cup Oak.
A stately tree 80 feet or more tall with a broad, rounded crown formed by stout branches and a straight trunk 3 feet in diameter.

Leaves — Alternate, simple, deciduous. Thick and firm, dark green and shiny on top, paler and somewhat hairy beneath. Roughly violin-shaped in general outline, ½ to 1 foot long, 3 to 6 inches wide.

Flowers — In spring, male catkins 4 to 6 inches in length usually borne from last year's wood, whereas the female flowers are at the base of the new leaves.

Fruit — Maturing in the fall. The large acorns, 1 inch long or

109

more, are enclosed in a thick cup with a fringed, rugged margin which gives the tree its common name.

Twigs — Thick and stout, brown, often developing corky ridges down to the small branches but not noticeable on the larger branches. Terminal buds conical or ovoid, ⅓ to ¼ inch long, reddish brown.

Bark — Dark gray to brown with prominent parallel vertical ridges and deep furrows.

Bur Oak is generally found along stream bottoms and adjacent slopes in North and East Central Texas. The wood is comparable to White Oak and is used for many of the same purposes. As an ornamental, Bur Oak has many endearing qualities. It is not particular as to site, is very hardy, and it tolerates drought and city smoke. The thick corky bark enables this tree to withstand fire and weedeater damage better than most oaks. The drought resistance is largely due to the deep taproot it develops at an early age. Seedlings have been found to have a 4½ foot taproot at the end of the first growing season and eight-year-old plants may have 14-foot taproots. Although the deep root system makes these trees difficult to transplant, that, together with the thick fire-resistant bark, enables them to successfully compete with prairie grasses and shrubs.

In the fringe areas between prairie and forest, Bur Oaks often form areas of widely-spaced trees with a ground cover of grasses and shrubs. In the landscape this tree can become large and dominating. It provides a deep shade, has few insect or disease problems, and in winter the corky twigs and stout branches give it a picturesque appearance. The large acorns are sought after by wildlife and can be eaten by humans if they are leached or parched. This is one of our most distinct and interesting trees, deserving more attention for shade or park plantings. Our state champion Bur Oak is 75 feet tall, 252 inches in circumference, and has a crown spread of 106 feet. It grows in the Denison Dam area, Cooke County.

WHITE OAK

Quercus alba.
Outstanding long-lived deciduous tree over 100 feet tall and 3 feet in diameter with heavy spreading branches forming a broad round-topped crown and a short trunk.

Leaves — Alternate, simple, firm, smooth, 4 to 9 inches in length. Dark green above, paler beneath, turning reddish in the fall.

Flowers — In early spring, male catkins 3 inches long in hanging clusters, female flowers in inconspicuous catkins at the tips of the current year's growth.

112

Fruit — Acorns maturing in one year ripening in the fall, about 1 inch long, germinating in the fall.
Twigs — Slender to stout, hairy and green to reddish brown when young, becoming smooth and gray later. The pith is star-shaped in cross section.
Bark — Gray and thin, somewhat scaly at first, becoming darker and furrowed with age.

White Oak is commonly found in forests of the East Texas Piney Wood region westward to Red River, Cass, Anderson, and Harris counties. The wood is heavy, hard, and is the most important of the white oak group. It is the favored wood for whiskey barrels because of its impermeability and for railroad ties due to its durability. Other common uses are flooring (resistant to abrasion), firewood, and boat building. The wood is noted for its attractive grain and its ability to finish smoothly and to hold nails well.

This is a prized lawn and shade tree but the growth is somewhat slow and it is difficult to transplant due to its deep taproot (first year seedlings 4 inches tall may have a taproot up to ½ inch in diameter and 18 inches deep). Early pioneers looked for White Oaks as indicators of fertile soils for farming. The acorns are rich in fat and protein. They were a staple of the American Indian diet. Although they are not as bitter as red oak acorns they still must be boiled to eliminate the tannic acid. This can be done by removing the shells, boiling the kernels, and changing the water until it remains clear. The nuts are eaten by a number of wildlife species and the leaves are browsed by livestock. White Oak is the state tree of Connecticut and Maryland.

Fagaceae - Beech Family

OVERCUP OAK

Quercus lyrata.
Moderate sized deciduous tree to about 60 feet tall with a small irregular crown and a trunk to 3 feet in diameter.

Leaves — Alternate, simple, 6 to 10 inches in length, 3 to 6 inches wide, dark green on top, lighter and somewhat hairy beneath.

Flowers — In spring, male catkins about 2 inches long, female flowers in short spikes about ½ inch in length.

Fruit — Maturing the fall of the first year, very distinctive acorn cup which almost entirely covers the nut.

Twigs — Slender, gray, with rounded buds.

Bark — Ash gray to reddish brown with longitudinal ridges.

114

Overcup Oak is a typical member of the flora found in swamps and river bottoms throughout the Piney Woods region of East Texas. The wood is not quite as good as, but is very similar to, White Oak and is used for the same purposes. This tree is fairly slow growing and long-lived but is not used very often as an ornamental because of its poor growth form. The acorns are eaten by a number of water-

fowl and other wildlife species; they can be utilized by humans as a survival food but the tannins must be leached out first. The state champion Overcup Oak is located in the Longhorn Army Ammunition Depot near Marshall. It is 216 inches in circumference, 88 feet tall, and has a crown spread of 81 feet.

LIVE OAK

Quercus virginiana.
Encino.
Large spreading evergreen tree to about fifty feet tall with a crown of up to one hundred feet in diameter.

Leaves — Thick, shiny, dark green above, lighter below. One to three inches long, ½ to 1 inch wide. Margins entire or spine toothed. Falling in early spring.

Flowers — Male and female flowers borne in separate catkins on a tree. Male catkins 2 to 3½ inches long, hairy with a yellow calyx; female catkins 1 to 3 inches long with 3 red stigmas.

Fruit — Acorns about 1 inch long, cup somewhat narrowed at the base.

Twigs — Brittle, grayish white to brown, tomentose when young becoming smooth and glabrous later.

Bark — Gray and smooth at first, becoming darker and furrowed with age.

116

Live Oak is found along the Coastal Plains and into the South Central Texas region. It is very resistant to salt spray and proliferates in coastal areas where many other plants are eliminated. The wood is very heavy, hard, and strong. This tree was formerly very important in shipbuilding and furnished some of the wood for "Old Ironsides."

Due to their longevity and majestic nature, Live Oaks mark the spot of many important events in Texas history. The wounded General Sam Houston was in repose under a Live Oak when he accepted Santa Anna's surrender at the San Jacinto battlefield. They are often planted as ornamentals outside their range for their sturdy evergreen nature. The acorns are rich in oil and are eaten by almost

every creature where they are found. The oak wilt fungus, which is devastating Live Oaks in the Hill Country, is not as great a problem on this coastal species. *Q. fusiformis*, however, have been hard hit. Our state champion Live Oak is probably one of the biggest trees in Texas. It is 44 feet tall, has a trunk circumference of 422 inches and a crown spread of 89 feet, and grows in Aransas County at Goose Island State Park near Rockport.

PLATEAU LIVE OAK. *Quercus fusiformis.*

Differs in having narrowed acorn cups and an inland range from Northern Mexico and Central Texas to Oklahoma. It can be found on any site except the very wet or dry. Both this species and the coastal one will often spread from root sprouts giving rise to colonies or "motts." This has been costly where the oak wilt fungus is present as the disease can spread from tree to tree through the connected roots, wiping out entire colonies and leaving behind a fearful scene of stark devastation. Recent evidence indicates Live Oaks may grow faster than formerly believed and many of the really large trees are not ancient but only old.

SCRUB OAK. *Quercus pungens.*

Shrubs or small trees about 25 feet tall found on the lower slopes and along canyon edges in the Trans-Pecos mountains. It can be recognized by its many-toothed shiny evergreen leaves that have a somewhat sandpapery feel to the upper surface.

VASEY OAK. *Quercus pungens* var. *vaseyana.*

Shrubs or small trees about 25 feet tall found on hillsides and canyon edges in Central and West Texas. Differs from the above species by having a smooth upper leaf surface, fewer marginal teeth, and only partially evergreen. It is often mistaken for Live Oak where they grow together but differs by having thinner leaves with more teeth, somewhat deciduous, and the bark is silvery scaly whereas Live Oak has darker furrowed bark.

ARIZONA WHITE OAK. *Quercus arizonica*

Small, mostly evergreen tree that can be seen in Hueco Tanks State Park near El Paso.

GRAY OAK

Quercus grisea.
Shin oak, Scrub Oak. An evergreen shrub or medium sized tree found on dry, gravelly soils in the mountains of West Texas.

Leaves — Leathery, gray green, ½ to 2 inches long, entire or toothed toward the tip. Slight fuzz on upper and under-side of leaf.

Flowers — Female in short spikes, male catkins ¾ to 1¼ inch long.

Fruit — Acorns singly or in pairs, light brown, ½ inch long, about ⅓ enclosed by cup.

Twigs — Slender, gray, often covered with a light brown fuzz.

Bark — Dark gray, deeply furrowed with age.

119

This is a common evergreen oak throughout the mountains of West Texas, usually low growing and shrubby on open gravelly hillsides but occasionally attaining heights of 60 feet under favorable conditions. It is one of the dominant trees of the *encinal* or live oak formation of West Texas. The dusty gray foliage gives it its name. The Gray Oak is very similar in appearance to Mohr Oak, except that the leaves of Mohr Oak are green and shiny above with whitish hairs on the undersides, while Gray Oak leaves are hairy on both surfaces. The Gray Oak is found in soils of igneous

origin while the Mohr Oak usually grows on limestone soils. Occasionally the ranges overlap, making identification difficult because these two oaks are known to hybridize. The Gray Oak wood is used for fence posts and fuel. The leaves are browsed by deer and livestock. Birds, squirrels, and javelina eat the acorns.

MOHR OAK. *Quercus mohriana.*

A low-growing shrub or small tree of West and West Central Texas growing on dry limestone hills and mesas, distinguished from Gray Oak by having dark green, shiny leaves, sparsely hairy above and a duller undersurface with gray to whitish hairs. The Gray Oak has gray-green leaves, hairy on the upper and under surface.

120

EMORY OAK

Quercus emoryi.
Black Oak.
An evergreen tree with a rounded crown usually under 50 feet tall.

Leaves — Partly evergreen, ¾ to 3 inches long, stiff, dark green and glossy above, paler and sometimes hairy beneath; leaf margin smooth or toothed.

121

Fagaceae - Beech Family

Flowers — Female flower a short spike; male catkins hairy, yellow, 1-2 inches long.
Fruit — Acorns single or paired; oblong, pointed at the tip, ½ inch long, dark brown, ⅓ to ½ enclosed in a scaly, often hairy cup. Ripen in August or September.
Twigs — Reddish brown, hairy; becoming smooth later.
Bark — Thick, dark brown to black; broken into large oblong plates by deep fissures on older trees.

The Emory Oak is fairly abundant at elevations above 4,500 feet in canyons, moist valleys, and creek bottoms in the Chisos and Davis mountains. The tree is named in honor of William H. Emory who conducted a survey of the United States-Mexican border in 1857. The Emory Oak is an attractive tree with toothed leaf margins giving it a holly-like appearance. It is nearly evergreen; the leaves drop gradually in the spring with new foliage appearing soon after. The wood of Emory Oak is used mainly for fuel. Deer, turkey, quail, and chipmunks relish the sweet acorns.

These acorns have been used as a source of flour in Mexico and by Indians of the Southwest. The acorns are boiled for a few hours, the water changed regularly to remove the bitter tannic acid. Indians occasionally placed baskets filled with acorns in a stream for a few days to leach off the tannins. They can then be ground into a flour or meal having a sweet, nutty flavor. Emory Oak is thought to hybridize with Chisos Red Oak, Scrub Oak, and Silverleaf Oak.

SILVERLEAF OAK. *Quercus hypoleucoides.*

Medium sized tree to about 35 feet tall with a rounded, conical crown, the lower branches somewhat pendant toward the tips. Fairly rare in Texas, this tree is found only as scattered populations at the higher elevations of the Davis Mountains in Jeff Davis County. It is easily distinguished

from other oaks by its narrow, 2- to 4-inch-long leaves that are dark green above and densely covered with silvery white below. This tree will often hybridize with Chisos Red Oak *Q. gravesii* to form the Livermore Oak *Q.* x *inconstans.*

WILLOW OAK

Quercus phellos.
A large handsome tree to 80 feet tall or more with a somewhat conical crown, the lower branches drooping slightly, becoming more rounded at maturity. The straight trunk can reach diameters in excess of 2-3 feet.

Leaves — Alternate, deciduous, turning pale yellow in the fall, 2-4 inches long and about 1 inch or less wide, shiny and light green on the upper surface, smooth or slightly hairy and dull below. Juvenile foliage is rarely lobed.

124

Flowers — In spring with the new leaves, the sexes separate but on the same tree. Male flowers in hairy drooping catkins 2-3 inches long; the female flowers tiny and borne in several flowered clusters from the leaf axils.

Fruit — Ripening in mid fall of the second year as ½-inch-long, rounded acorns in shallow cups enclosing about ¼ of the total length of the nut.

Twigs — Slender and smooth, reddish brown at first, turning gray with age, the terminal buds up to ⅛ inch long.

Bark — Thin and tight, gray and somewhat smooth at first, becoming roughened and darker with maturity and eventually almost black.

Willow Oak is usually found in bottomlands associated with rivers, creeks, and major streams throughout East Texas west to Bastrop County. The strong and coarse-grained wood is similar to red oak and is used for many of the same purposes, such as pallets, rough construction, railroad ties, and firewood. Willow Oak is an excellent shade tree for East Texas with its relatively fast growth, lustrous foliage, and high-branching crown. It has few serious pest or disease problems but the thin bark is easily damaged and trees on dry sites grow poorly. Large Willow Oaks are frequently found around old homesteads in East Texas or as street plantings in older neighborhoods. Many species of wildlife that frequent bottomland situations rely on the abundant acorn crop as a food source.

125

LAUREL OAK. *Quercus laurifolia.*

This name now also includes DIAMOND LEAF OAK. *Q. obtusa.*

A large tree 80 feet or more tall, found in river bottoms or swampy sites in East Texas from Sabine and Leon to Harris and Orange counties with a disjunct population in Henderson County. This tree is similar to Willow Oak but differs by having wider, almost evergreen, foliage over 1 inch long that is often lobed on young trees. Laurel Oak also prefers somewhat wetter sites. It has many of the same desirable shade tree characteristics as Willow Oak such as fast growth, a compact crown, and shiny leaves; the wood is not as good because it checks badly when drying, but it still makes great firewood. The state champion Laurel Oak is in the Alabama-Coushatta Indian Reservation near Livingston. It is 124 feet tall and has a trunk girth of 93 inches and a crown spread of 76 feet.

COASTAL LAUREL OAK. *Quercus hemisphaerica.*

A small tree to about 30 feet tall or a clump-forming shrub found in sandy soil near streams along the coast from Calhoun and Victoria counties southwest to Nueces County.

WATER OAK

Quercus nigra.
Medium sized or large tree about 30 feet tall with a symmetrical rounded crown and a trunk 2 to 3 feet in diameter.

Leaves — Alternate, simple, deciduous but usually hanging on until Christmas in normal winters. Dull blue green above and paler beneath. Quite variable but most often 2 to 4 inches long and typically three-lobed but can be entire or pinnately lobed.

Fagaceae - Beech Family

Flowers — In spring, male flowers in catkins 2 to 3 inches in length, female flowers in short spikes consisting of only a few individuals.

Fruit — Single or paired, and maturing the second season. The black nut is about ½ inch long, often with vertical lighter colored lines, finely hairy in a thin saucer-like cup.

Twigs — Slender, smooth, dark red with a reddish-brown, sharp-pointed terminal bud up to ¼ inch in length.

Bark — Light brown to dark grayish black, smooth and thin but later developing rough, wide scaly ridges.

Water Oak is commonly found along streams and river bottoms but also in moist upland woods throughout the eastern third of Texas west to the Colorado River area. The wood is generally considered not as good as many other oaks and is usually used for the same purposes as Red Oak. Water oak is fast growing and transplants easily. It has few serious pests and diseases and grows on a wide variety of sites. These features make it a very popular ornamental shade tree in East and Southeast Texas. The acorns are eaten by many species of wildlife from ducks to turkeys and squirrels.

128

SANDJACK OAK

Quercus incana.
Bluejack Oak.
A large shrub or small tree to about 30 feet tall, with stout crooked branches forming an irregular spreading crown and a short trunk 20 inches in diameter.

Leaves— Alternate, firm, falling off late in the fall, 2 to 5 inches long and ½ to 1½ inches wide. New leaves are pink and hairy, older ones are dark green on top with dense, grayish-green hair on the underside.

129

Fagaceae - Beech Family

Flowers — In spring, male catkins 2 to 3 inches long, the female flowers small, single or sometimes paired.
Fruit — Maturing the second year, rounded, about ½ inch in diameter, nuts with yellowish lines especially on the lower half.
Twigs — Thin, somewhat ribbed, grayish hairy.
Bark — Reddish brown to black, usually spotted with light blotches of lichens, broken into rough small blocks.

Sandjack Oak is generally restricted to dry, upland sandy areas in East and Central Texas. It has very few desirable qualities either as an ornamental or for commercial use. The wood is used for firewood and fence posts. Wildlife feed on the acorns, and the trees often form dense thickets providing valuable cover on otherwise barren sandy habitats. The national champion Sandjack Oak is located in the Angelina National Forest. It is 75 inches in circumference, 50 feet tall, and has a crown spread of 55 feet.

AMERICAN ELM

Ulmus americana.
An attractive tree about 80 feet tall with a symmetrical crown of spreading branches that arch and droop at the tips. The buttressed trunk, 2 to 3 feet thick, usually divides into several large ascending branches. The overall form of open-grown American Elms is often likened to a column or fountain of water. Trees in Central Texas tend to have shorter, more broadly rounded, crowns.

Leaves — Alternate, simple, deciduous, 3 to 6 inches long, new growth very rough on top surface when rubbed in the direction toward the tip, dark green and smooth when mature, paler and hairy below, coarsely double-toothed on the margin. Turning yellow in the fall.

131

Flowers — Appearing before the leaves in very early spring, small and perfect on thin hanging stalks.

Fruit — Maturing in spring or early summer, in hanging clusters of 3 to 5, slightly less than ½ inch long, consisting of a single seed surrounded by a wing. Usually produced in abundance.

Twigs — Slender, new growth light green and downy, later becoming smooth and reddish brown; the lack of a true terminal bud gives them a zigzag appearance.

Bark — Ash gray to dark brown, broken into deep fissures and flat-topped ridges which alternate light and dark bands in cross section.

American Elm is most often found near streams and rivers as well as in adjacent moist woods throughout East and Central Texas extending south and westward to Bexar and Coke counties. It is fast growing, reasonably long-lived, and grows on a wide variety of sites. Easily transplanted, it has a beautiful shape when allowed to develop in the open. On the other hand, the roots are fairly shallow, causing them to dry out quickly on thin soils, and making it difficult to grow other plants under them. Trees in prairie areas tend to develop a wind-swept look due to the prevailing breezes.

Elms in general are subject to several disease problems, with Dutch Elm disease being the most important. In Texas, these problems are not as frequent as in other areas, so planting them here may not be as risky as many believe, especially in areas with good soil and ample water. Even though the ascending branches are susceptible to damage from severe ice storms, the wood is considered moderately hard, heavy, and strong, with an interlocking grain that makes it difficult to split. The thick sapwood is yellowish with distinct growth rings and the heartwood is light brown often tinged with red. It was formerly used for ship blocks, wheel hubs, yokes, barrel hoops, and was considered one

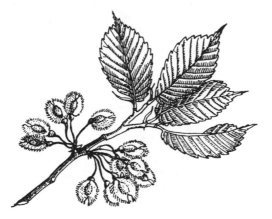

of the best woods for barrel staves. The main uses now are for railroad ties, boxes, and crates; because of its good bending qualities, it is often used for the arching or curved parts of furniture. The bark was made into cord and also used for chair bottoms. American Elm seeds are eaten by many species of birds and rodents; the foliage and buds are browsed by deer and rabbits. The state champion American Elm is owned by the State Department of Highways and Public Transportation and is located in Wood County. It is 192 inches in circumference, 99 feet tall, and has a crown spread of 92 feet. American Elm is the state tree of Massachusetts, Nebraska, and North Dakota.

SIBERIAN ELM. *Ulmus pumila.*

Small to moderate short-lived tree about 40 feet tall with a rounded crown and somewhat drooping twigs. Frequently planted as street and shade trees in dry areas because of its drought resistance. Introduced from Asia but escaping from cultivation in the western half of Texas and other areas. The leaves are usually single-toothed whereas our other native elms have double-toothed margins.

WATER ELM. *Planera aquatica.*
Planer Tree.

A small tree about 25 feet tall with slender branches, an open crown, and a trunk 1 foot in diameter. Usually found in swamps, along streams, and at the edge of lakes and rivers in East Texas west to Brazos and Matagorda counties. The 2-inch-long leaves are dull dark green above, paler

beneath with yellowish veins, and are single-toothed, whereas true elms have double teeth on the margins. The fruit is single seeded, about ½ inch long, and covered with fleshy projections. The bark is covered with large gray to light brown scales that peel back to reveal the red-brown inner bark. The state champion Water Elm is located in the Davy Crockett National Forest near Crockett. It is 36 feet tall and has a trunk circumference of 121 inches and a crown spread of 55 feet.

SLIPPERY ELM

Ulmus rubra.
Red Elm.
A moderate sized tree to about 70 feet tall with branches spreading to form a broad, open, flat-topped crown and a tall straight trunk 2 feet in diameter.

Leaves — Alternate, simple, deciduous, thick and coarse, 5 to 9 inches in length. Dark green, very rough and sand-

135

papery on top surface when rubbed in both directions, paler and somewhat hairy beneath, turning yellow in the fall.

Flowers — In early spring, short stalked, few flowered clusters, small, perfect, reddish.

Fruit — Maturing in late spring or early summer, a single seed entirely surrounded by a small wing, ⅜ to ⅞ inch long.

Twigs — Thicker than American Elm, flexible, greenish brown and distinctly fuzzy at first, becoming smooth with age. The false terminal bud creates a zigzag effect with the twigs; buds are about ⅓ inch long, dark chestnut brown or almost black with red-brown hairs that are very conspicuous as the buds are swelling in the spring.

Bark — Gray to red brown, becoming about one inch thick with deep furrows and parallel, more or less continuous, ridges that are somewhat flattened; in cross section the ridges are solid brown whereas American Elm bark alternates light and dark bands.

Slippery Elm is usually found on moist hills associated with creeks, streams, and rivers in East and Central Texas westward to about Kerr and Comanche counties. The wood is similar to American Elm but has a heartwood that is more reddish brown and is easier to split. It generally warps easily if not stored properly and is used commercially as a "soft elm." Slippery Elm grows faster than American Elm, is easy to transplant, and even though it is susceptible to many of the same diseases as its cousin it still makes an attractive shade tree on good sites with rich soil.

The common name comes from the shiny, thick, white inner bark next to the wood. This layer forms a gummy mass when chewed and was used by the early settlers for many purposes — best known as a thirst quencher and for soothing sore throats. Long strips of the bark were peeled off in the spring and dried; later, when moistened, this was used for wound dressings and poultices for carbuncles and boils. It also makes a pleasant wholesome tea after steeping in hot water for about 15 minutes. Dried and ground, the inner bark also makes a nutritious flour. Many health-food stores still carry Slippery Elm. The rough fibrous nature made it useful cordage for rope, chairs, thongs, and lacings. Squirrels, other small rodents, and some birds eat the seeds but they are not an important wildlife food.

CEDAR ELM

Ulmus crassifolia.
Olmo.
A medium sized tree to 60 feet tall
with a narrow, rounded crown and
often with a buttressed trunk 2 feet
in diameter.

Leaves — Alternate, simple, deciduous, 1 to 2 inches in length,
   dark green and rough above, paler beneath, stiff-toothed
   margins, turning yellow in fall.

138

Flowers — Small perfect flowers appear in late summer or fall in short-stalked clusters at the leaf bases. This is our only native autumn-flowering elm.

Fruit — Maturing in late summer to early fall, a single seed entirely surrounded by a wing, a total length of about ⅜ inch.

Twigs — Slender reddish brown, often drooping, minutely hairy at first turning smooth later, slightly zigzagged in appearance. Young branchlets frequently have paired parallel corky ridges, called wings, on the sides.

Bark — Light brown, tinged with red, somewhat thickish with broad ridges separating deep furrows.

Cedar Elm grows on a wide variety of soils from dry limestone ridges to river bottoms where it reaches its greatest size and dominates level areas known as "Cedar Elm flats." This is the most widespread native elm species in Texas. It is found from the Pecos River in the west to the southern tip and to the northeast corner of the state. Olmos, the Spanish term for these trees, has been used in naming a number of sites, such as Olmos Park in San Antonio and the town of Olmo in South Texas. A hardy tree that grows reasonably fast, it is easily transplanted, requires little care, and will tolerate drought and seasonally wet areas. These features have made it a popular landscape and shade tree in many parts of Texas, particularly those areas with limestone soils. One drawback is that it often develops an irregular, unsymmetrical crown. Other problems are that trees under severe stress are subject to red spider infestations and the shallow root system can be a problem when trying to grow plants near them. Branches often break or split in windstorms and the fall-borne pollen causes some people serious allergy reactions.

Cedar Elm wood is hard and heavy but usually knotty and difficult to split, making it poor firewood. The small fruits are usually abundant but are only of minor importance to wildlife such as squirrels, mice, and turkeys. The state champion Cedar Elm is near Oletha in Limestone County. It is 98 inches in circumference, 94 feet tall, and has a crown spread of 50 feet.

WINGED ELM

Ulmus alata.
Medium sized tree to about 40 feet tall with an open, round-topped crown and a straight trunk 18 inches in diameter.

Leaves — Alternate, deciduous, 1 to 2½ inches long, smooth on top and slightly hairy below, the margins coarsely toothed. Turning yellow before dropping in the fall.

Flowers — In early spring, before the leaves appear, perfect, petalless in few flowered clusters. Individual flowers dark reddish brown about ⅛ inch long with 5 stamens.

Fruit — Ripening in late spring as a small single seed surrounded by a hairy wing notched at the tip, the whole thing about ¼ inch long.

141

Ulmaceae - Elm Family

Twigs — Slender, somewhat zigzag due to the lack of a true terminal bud, brown and smooth with scaly, chestnut-brown pointed buds about ⅛ inch long. The twigs often develop bizarre flattened corky projections which resemble "wings" in some instances.

Bark — Thin, brown, and somewhat smooth at first but soon breaking into longitudinal fissures and flat-topped ridges.

Winged Elm is a handsome tree in cultivation resembling a dwarf version of its cousin, the stately American Elm. In nature it is found throughout the East Texas Piney Woods and on sandy soils west through the Post Oak Belt. It usually appears as scattered individuals on all but the wettest or driest sites. The wood is like other "hard elms", being heavy and difficult to split, thus well suited for tool handles, wheel hubs, and furniture pieces such as table legs. Early settlers used the fibrous inner bark as cordage for tying cotton or hay bales.

Winged Elm reliably produces abundant fruit crops that are eaten by a number of birds and squirrels which also eat the buds. The fruits generally ripen so early they are available before almost anything else, making them important in their own right. This is a good sturdy ornamental tree for today's small lots and roadsides. It is not prone to any special problems, has a good growth form, and does not generate any particular annoying litter to contend with; however, it does have somewhat shallow roots which make growing other plants under it somewhat difficult.

142

SUGARBERRY

Celtis laevigata.
Sugar Hackberry.
Medium sized tree to 70 feet tall with a broad rounded crown and a single straight or short trunk to 2 feet thick that soon divides into upright arching branches.

Leaves — Alternate, simple, deciduous, 1½ to 3 inches in length, dark green above, paler beneath, usually widest below the middle with an unequal base and a smooth margin or with a few teeth present.

Flowers — In spring, small, green, inconspicuous and perfect.
Fruit — Ripening in summer, about ⅛ inch in diameter, with a thin sweet edible orange-red to yellow flesh.
Twigs — Slender, light green at first, later becoming reddish brown with a small, white, chambered pith visible when cut longitudinally. Buds are small, chestnut brown, and hairy.
Bark — Gray, thin, and smooth with scattered corky warts or corky broken ridges covering the trunk giving it an extremely rough texture.

Sugarberry is surely one of the most common trees in the eastern third of Texas. It is frequently found on clay soils in stream and river bottoms but can be discovered on virtually any site throughout its range. The wood is pale yellow with distinct annual rings and is similar to Elm in texture and structure, but is mostly sapwood and rots quickly. Sugarberry grows fast, gives good shade, is easily transplanted, tolerates a very wide range of soils and climatic conditions, is resistant to city pollution, has a shallow root system that holds the soil, and like other *Celtis* species is resistant to Texas cotton root rot.

Most tree experts consider *Celtis* in general as undesirable weedy pests because of their ragged appearance, habit of reseeding in abundance, shallow invasive root system, thin, easily-damaged bark, many minor problems that render the foliage of young branches unsightly at times, and the quickness of the wood to decay. Nevertheless, they are a good selection to plant in areas where nothing else will grow. The sweet-fleshed fruits are produced in abundance and are a favorite food of many species of birds.

HACKBERRY. *Celtis occidentalis.*

A medium sized tree to 50 feet that in Texas is restricted to the Panhandle area and differs from other *Celtis* species by typically having sharply-toothed leaf margins.

NETLEAF HACKBERRY. *Celtis reticulata.*
Palo Blanco.

A tree to about 30 feet tall that is, in Texas, mostly restricted to north central, central, and south parts but has some isolated locations in the east and west. It differs from other species by having thicker leaves with raised netlike veins on the lower surface of the leaf. It has a more western distribution than Sugarberry, and where it is found with Hackberry the leaves are entire or with a few scattered teeth on the margins.

LINDHEIMER HACKBERRY. *Celtis lindheimeri.*

A small tree found only in Central and South Texas. It differs from other Hackberries by being uniformly covered with soft hairs on the leaf undersurface. The national champion Lindheimer Hackberry is located in Comal County and is 72 inches in circumference, 43 feet tall, and has a crown spread of 46 feet.

DWARF HACKBERRY. *Celtis tenuifolia.*

A small tree to 20 feet tall found in Southeast Texas that differs from our other native species by having thin, somewhat smaller, leaves and a dwarf stature.

GRANJENO. *Celtis pallida.*
Spiny Hackberry, Palo Blanco.

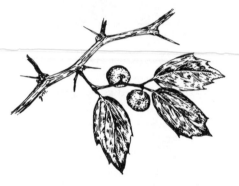

A shrubby plant with zigzag spiny branches, leaves ½ to 2 inches long, often toothed at the tip. Fruit is orange to yellow, ⅓ to ½ inches across, juicy, and edible. The plant is native to brushland in South, Central, and West Texas. The leaves and branches of this plant are very high in crude protein and are readily browsed by livestock.

146

OSAGE-ORANGE

Maclura pomifera.
Horse Apple, Bois D'Arc, Bodark,
Hedge Apple.
Moderate sized tree about 40 feet tall
with an open, irregular crown and a
short trunk to 3 feet in diameter.

Leaves — Alternate, simple, deciduous, 3 to 6 inches in length,
bright green and shiny, turning clear yellow in fall.
Flowers — In spring to early summer, sexes on separate plants.
Male flowers small and greenish in many flowered elongated clusters at the leaf bases; female flowers also small
and greenish, at the leaf bases in rounded clusters.
Fruit — Very distinctive, rounded, about 5 inches thick, green
but turning yellowish when ripe, the surface covered
with bumps and convolutions somewhat resembling a
brain, juice milky with many seeds found throughout the
flesh of the fruit.
Twigs — Slender, turning light orange brown with a stout thorn

147

at the leaf base up to 1 inch long, the milky sap turning black when dry.

Bark — Light orange brown, thin when young, becoming thicker with broad longitudinal ridges peeling into strips separated by irregular furrows.

This tree is native to East and Central Texas but is now found throughout Texas along creeks, streams, and fence lines. Most people know it as Horse Apple or Bodark. The name Bodark comes from the French words *bois d'arc,* meaning "wood of the bow", because the arching branches were a favorite among Osage Indians and others for bow wood. The hard, heavy wood is very resistant to decay. In the past it was so renowned for its durability that in some areas of Central Texas, house loans were refused unless the wooden structure rested on Bodark piers. It makes excellent fence posts but is not recommended for firewood as it pops continuously, sending sparks flying. Pioneers utilized the tough wood for wagon-wheel hubs. The wood is bright orange with a thin, lighter colored sapwood. The root bark is the source of a yellow or tan dye used for dying wool, while the trunk bark was formerly employed in tanning leather. The name Hcdge Apple refers to the use of these trees as living fences and impenetrable hedge rows before the advent of barbed wire. During this period the tree became widely cultivated and naturalized outside of its native range.

These trees grow reasonably fast, transplant easily, are fairly resistant to pests and disease (except Texas cotton root rot) and will tolerate many different soil types including dry or moist sites. On the other hand, the trees tend to have a coarse growth habit and the large fruits can be a chore to clean up in the fall. A thornless and fruitless male clone variety is now available in the nursery trade. Recent studies seem to support the old belief that a portion of the fruit placed around the house will repel roaches. Few animals eat the fruit, but squirrels and bobwhite quail are known to eat the seeds. It is said that squirrels reach a state of intoxication after eating the fermented fruits.

RED MULBERRY

Morus rubra.
Small to medium sized trees 30 to 40 feet tall with a spreading flattened crown and a short trunk to about 2 feet thick.

Leaves — Alternate, simple, deciduous, 3-5 inches long, rough hairy on top and soft and hairy below. Leaves variable especially on vigorous young shoots. Classically almost heart-shaped but often somewhat mitten-shaped or sometimes deeply 3- 5-lobed on young sucker shoots. Turning yellow in the fall.

Flowers — In spring, the sexes on separate trees, male flowers in drooping cylindrical spikes 2 to 3 inches long, females borne the same but only about 1 inch in length.

Fruit — Ripening in early to midsummer, many small juicy fruits clustered together that look like a stretched out blackberry. Red when green but turning purple when mature.

150

Twigs — Stout, smooth, greenish brown tinged with red, without a true terminal bud, causing them to be slightly zigzagged, somewhat swollen at the nodes; the buds are about ⅖ inch long and covered with prominent scales. The sap is a milky juice.

Bark — Begins to develop early; about the third year it starts to split longitudinally and diagonally, becoming dark grayish brown and peeling off in long narrow flakes at maturity.

Red Mulberry is found throughout East and Central Texas in stream and creek bottoms and moist woods. The wood is reddish with a thin yellowish sapwood. Mulberry lumber, although uncommon and usually small, is fairly attractive. It is mostly used for fence posts because of its durability in the soil.

The fruits are delicious but the competition with songbirds, who will eat them while still green, is intense. (This may account for their lack of widespread popularity as jams, jellies, or drinks.) The new shoot growth as it unfolds is good as a vegetable if cooked for about 20 minutes. Red Mulberries have a good growth rate, an attractive spreading form, are easily transplanted, tolerate some shade, are fairly drought and pollution resistant, and are relatively free of serious pests or disease. They do best with a lot of room to develop their spreading crowns. Female trees should never be planted where the purple-juiced berries or the accompanying bird droppings (similarly colored) will be a problem. It is said that the unripe fruits and green shoots contain hallucinogens. In East Texas, the leafing out of Red Mulberry is said to indicate all danger of frost has passed.

151

LITTLE LEAF MULBERRY. *Morus microphylla.* Texas Mulberry.

Small tree about 20 feet tall, with smaller leaves to 2½ inches long and rough on both upper and lower surfaces. This dwarf version of Red Mulberry is found along creeks and in canyons of Central and West Texas. The wood is somewhat elastic and was made into bows by the Indians. The national champion Texas Mulberry is 25 feet tall and has a crown spread of 30 feet and a trunk circumference of 22 inches. It is located in Kerr County.

WHITE MULBERRY. *Morus alba.*

Differs from other Mulberries by having the leaves smooth on both sides, leaves more deeply lobed, and the fruit less tasty and pink or white when ripe. The tree is used extensively for windbreaks and shade plantings and has escaped cultivation, becoming fairly common around urban areas. It is a native to China where it is the favorite fodder for silkworms.

PAPER MULBERRY. *Broussonetia papyrifera.*

Medium sized tree about 30 feet tall with flowers borne in round balls rather than cylindrical spikes and large (3 to 8 inches in length) leaves that are rough on the upper surface and velvety hairy beneath. This tree is native to China and Japan and has been used extensively in the southern U.S. as an ornamental. It is fairly drought resistant but its tendency to sucker freely from the roots makes it undesirable for shade tree plantings. In its homeland the tree is known for the fibrous quality of the bark in the making of paper and cloth.

SOUTHERN MAGNOLIA

Magnolia grandiflora.
Bull Bay Magnolia.
Well-known, beautiful evergreen tree to 80 feet tall with a rounded or pyramidal crown and a thick straight trunk 2 to 3 feet in diameter.

Leaves — Alternate, simple, evergreen but dropping the second year. Thick and leathery, dark green and glossy above, rusty brown hairy beneath, 5 to 10 inches long, 3 to 5 inches in width.

153

Flowers — Late spring to midsummer, 6 to 12 large white petals opening 6 to 9 inches across; very fragrant.

Fruit — Ripening in the fall, cylindrical rusty brown cone, 2 to 4 inches long, bearing many shiny red seeds about ⅜ inch in length.

Twigs — Stout, covered with rusty brown hairs at first, terminal buds large, 1 to 1½ inches long, pale or covered with brown fur.

Bark — Tight, thin, and smooth at first, later becoming scaly, light brown to gray.

Southern Magnolia is to many people the symbol of the South. In Texas it grows naturally along streams and wet woods from Shelby County northeast of Nacogdoches south to Harris County and west to the Brazos River Valley. The wood of Magnolia is whitish and has few desirable qualities commercially; consequently these handsome trees are felled largely for use as railroad ties and furniture. Magnolia was formerly important for venetian blinds because of its good finishing qualities and general freedom from warping and twisting. This tree is a favorite ornamental throughout its natural range and many other areas. It has a good

154

growth rate, is free of serious pest or disease problems, and tolerates city air pollution; however, it does not fare well in hot dry locations or sites with thin soils. The shiny foliage looks almost black on an overcast day and unpruned trees form a column of foliage from the ground up that can completely hide the trunk. Magnolias will tolerate some shade but the fragrant blooms are best appreciated on trees grown in the open. The red seeds are eaten by birds and squirrels. Old specimens in the wild are good "den trees" because they often have large rotted cavities which make ideal critter homes.

The Magnolia family is considered by some to be among the most primitive and ancient of flowering plants alive today. Fossils have been found which reveal that these plants were growing an estimated 60 million years ago. Southern Magnolia is the state flower of Louisiana and the state tree of Mississippi. Our state champion tree is 205 inches in trunk circumference, 96 feet tall, and has a crown spread of 71 feet. It is located in the Sam Houston National Forest.

Magnoliaceae - Magnolia Family

SWEETBAY

Magnolia virginiana.
Swamp Bay.
A semi-evergreen tree to about 50 feet
tall with a trunk to 2 feet in diameter,
often surrounded by smaller stems
suckering from the base.

Leaves — Simple, alternate, 4 to 6 inches long and 1 to 2 inches
wide. Light green and glossy above, whitish beneath,
fragrant when crushed. Semi-evergreen but dropping
the next spring.
Flowers — In spring and early summer, creamy white and sweet
scented with 9 to 12 petals forming a flower 2 to 3 inches
in diameter.
Fruit — Ripening in late summer-fall, a reddish woody cone

156

about 2 inches in length with many compartments that split open and give forth a bright-red flattened seed ½ inch long hanging on a slender thread.

Twigs — Round, green, and downy at first, turning reddish brown later. The large pith is solid but marked by alternating bands of dark and light colors. Winter buds are finely silky-white hairy with the terminal bud being ½ to ¾ inch long.

Bark — Smooth, tight, thin, gray colored, and fragrant when bruised.

Sweetbay is a swamp-loving species, most common in marshy seep areas associated with creeks and streams in the southern half of the Texas Piney Woods west to the Conroe area. Sweetbay is fairly disease-resistant, has a moderate growth rate, attractive foliage, and fragrant flowers which have been used as a perfume base. The leaves are very distinctive when they flash their white undersides in a breeze. It is a beautiful ornamental tree for areas in East Texas where water is plentiful. The seeds are not particularly important to wildlife but are eaten by a few birds and rodents. Sweetbay logs are commonly utilized by beavers for dam building and in some places it is known as Beaver Tree.

157

PYRAMID MAGNOLIA. *Magnolia pyramidata.*

A small deciduous tree to 30 feet tall with the leaves usually clustered at the branch tips. It is considered by some to be only a variety of *Magnolia fraseri* and is readily distinguished by the thin leaves that are broadest near the tip with two earlike lobes at the base. Pyramid Magnolia is not common anywhere within its natural range and in Texas is restricted to the area of Jasper and Newton counties. The national champion is located there. It is 76 inches in circumference, 60 feet tall and has a crown spread of 37 feet.

PAWPAW

Asimina triloba.
Custard Apple.
A small tree to about 20 feet tall with
a wide crown.

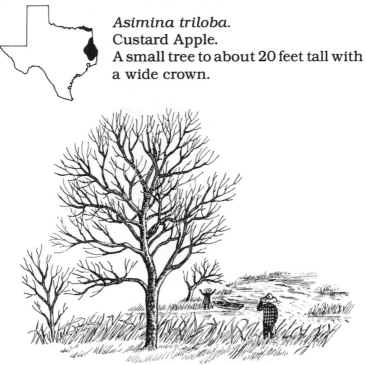

Leaves — Deciduous, thin, lightly reddish brown, hairy when
young, becoming smooth later. Light green ½ to 1 foot
long, 3-6 inches broad and somewhat odorous when
crushed.

Flowers — The exotic fleshy flowers are usually borne singly
in the leaf axils on wood of the previous season. They
open green and later turn purple, 1-2 inches across with
prominent veins.

Fruit — Edible, with a leathery skin and yellowish fleshy pulp,
1 to 2½ inches long and 1-2 large brown seeds inside.

Twigs — Gray or brown at first covered with fine dark red hairs,
becoming smooth with age. Winter buds naked but
covered with dark reddish brown hairs. Roundish flower
buds are often present on wood of the previous season.

Bark — Thin, smooth, gray to dark brown.

159

Pawpaw is a relatively fast growing, uncommon tree found in deep East and Northeast Texas. It is usually an understory tree associated with rich woods, creek valleys, and bottomlands where it often forms small colonies. This relative of the tropical Custard Apple has a very palatable fruit with a custard or banana-like flavor which can be made into various desserts. These tasty fruits are eagerly eaten by wildlife who rarely let them stay on the tree until fully ripened. A yellow dye can be made from the fruit pulp. Pawpaw is sometimes planted as an ornamental for its odd fleshy

flowers and large tropical-looking leaves that turn yellow in the fall. It does best in a moist situation that offers some protection from the wind which tears the lush foliage. The wood is light, soft, pulpy and yellowish-green in color. This tree has no serious pests or diseases.

REDBAY

Persea borbonia.
An attractive evergreen tree 30 feet or more tall with a dense, well-rounded crown and a short trunk 1 foot or so in diameter.

Leaves — Alternate, simple, dark green and leathery, falling the second year, bright green on the upper surface, somewhat whitish beneath, aromatic when crushed.

Flowers — In spring to early summer, white, bell-shaped, about ⅛ inch in length in the leaf axils; both sexes present on the same flower but petals are absent.

Fruit — Maturing in the fall, single-seeded, blue to almost black, up to ½ inch in diameter, borne on short stalks about ½ inch in length.

Twigs — Thin to moderately stout, green at first, often marked with dark mottling and turning brown as they get older.

Bark — Fairly thick, reddish brown, developing irregular furrows at a relatively early age.

161

Redbay is usually found growing in boggy situations and along streams and creeks in the southern half of the East Texas Piney Woods. It is also found in some of the deep sandy areas with Longleaf Pine, Yaupon, and Sandjack Oak. An isolated population can be found growing at Hamilton's Pool near Austin. The wood is attractive and would be good for cabinet work or paneling but the trees rarely reach a usable size. The fragrant foliage is used as "bay leaves" to flavor soups and stews. A few leaves were often stored with flour, meal, and other foods to act as an insect repellent.

Redbay has ornamental potential because of its moderate growth rate, relative freedom from pests and diseases, attractive foliage, and overall form. Some trees are attacked by a foliage gall which disfigures the leaves but otherwise does no harm.

The state champion Redbay is located in Camp Strake Boy Scout Camp at Conroe. It is 52 feet tall, 116 inches in circumference, and has a crown spread of 49 feet.

CAMPHOR TREE. *Cinnamomum camphora.*

Differs from Redbay by having leaves that smell strongly of camphor when crushed and leaf stalks that are usually 1 inch or more in length, whereas Red Bay has spicy fragrant leaves and leaf stalks usually less than 1 inch long. Camphor Tree is native to Asia but is planted as an ornamental along the coast and has naturalized in Southeast Texas. The wood of this tree is the commercial source of camphor for medicinal use.

SASSAFRAS

Sassafras albidum.
A medium sized deciduous tree to about 50 feet tall with a narrow open crown of horizontal branches and up-curved twigs and a short trunk 2 feet or more in diameter.

Leaves — Alternate, simple, deciduous, 3 to 6 inches in length and 2 to 4 inches wide. The leaf shapes vary but three distinct forms are most common: the simple shape, the single-lobed "mitten" style, or the 3 (rarely 5) lobed vari-

163

ation. All three types can often be found on the same tree. Suede green on top, paler beneath, turning bright orange, red, or salmon pink in the fall. Leaf stalks about 1 inch long.

Flowers — In early spring as the leaves unfold, greenish yellow and about ¼ inch wide in branched clusters about 2 inches long, quite attractive.

Fruit — Maturing in late summer, ¼ to ½ inch, round or oblong, shiny dark blue, single-seeded, fleshy, on coral red stalks about 1½ inch in length.

Twigs — Green, somewhat slender with a spicy taste and odor, rather brittle, buds about ¼ inch long, sharp pointed with a few greenish, loose-fitting bud scales.

Bark — Reddish and thin at first, becoming thick and developing a weathered gray or red brown color later with deep furrows and irregular flat ridges. Very distinctive at all ages.

Sassafras is common on sandy soils throughout East Texas west to Lamar, Brazos, and Harris counties. It is frequently found along fences and roads where it spreads prolifically from the roots and, together with Eastern Persimmon, is one of the first hardwood species to invade abandoned fields. Sassafras wood is sometimes used for paneling or cabinetmaking, as it resembles the more popular Ash (*Fraxinus* sp.). The fast growth rate, beautiful fall color, freedom from pests, and distinctive bark would make this an attractive ornamental but they are hard to transplant and young trees tend to sprout readily from the roots, creating thickets.

Indians had many uses for Sassafras, both medicinally and in cooking. Early European visitors readily accepted the natives' claims that the tree had special cure-all medicinal qualities. As a result, Sassafras became one of the first exported products from North America to Europe in 1602. The principal ingredient — oil of sassafras — is usually obtained by boiling the bark from the roots. Recently, however, Sassafras was found to cause cancer in laboratory test animals. Sassafras was widely used as a tea that allegedly purified or thinned the blood and was used in flavoring medicines, root beer, and candy. The leaves are still used today as "gumbo file" to thicken soups, predominantly in Cajun cooking. Sassafras fruits are a wildlife favorite. Fossils show that the genus Sassafras has been around for at least 50 million years. It once grew throughout what is now Greenland, North America, and Europe. Today it exists as three species confined to North America, China, and Taiwan.

WITCH HAZEL

Hamamelis virginiana.
Usually just a large shrub but sometimes a small tree to about 20 feet tall with several trunks and an irregular, rounded shape.

Leaves — Alternate, deciduous, about 2 to 6 inches long with an uneven base. Deep olive green above with prominent principal veins, paler below with hair along the veins, turning dull gold in the fall.

Flowers — Appearing when the leaves begin to drop in the fall. Very unusual in groups of 3, with 4 yellow narrow petals to 1 inch in length.

Fruit — Becoming ripe during the fall of the second season. The two-celled woody capsules persist over the winter after the seeds are gone. Seeds are torpedo-shaped, black and shiny. When the capsule dries out it bursts open and the seeds are shot out, often traveling several yards from the parent plant.

166

Twigs — Slender, somewhat zigzag and hairy becoming smoother by the end of the first year. The slightly flattened and club-shaped winter buds are about ½ inch in length, naked, hairy, and on short stalks.

Bark — Deep brown and smooth when young, becoming rather scaly when mature, often with lighter brown blotches and horizontal markings.

Witch Hazel is an interesting plant found in East and Central Texas. It is usually associated with creeks and streams as an understory plant. The yellow fall color, unusual flowers, pest-free nature, good growth rate, and nice form make Witch Hazel an attractive ornamental. It is probably best as a backdrop planting where its fall color and late flowers can be appreciated.

The name Witch Hazel refers to the notion that water diviners prefer branches from this plant for "witching" water. A medicinal extract is distilled from the bark and twigs, and used as an astringent rubbing lotion for soothing cuts, bruises, and mosquito bites. Witch Hazel is only moderately important to wildlife; the seeds are eaten by a few birds and the branches browsed by deer, rabbits, and squirrels.

VERNAL WITCH HAZEL. *Hamamelis vernalis.*

Differs from common Witch Hazel by blooming in late winter or early spring. The yellow, orange, and purple fall colors, along with its habit of blooming when very little else does, makes it a good ornamental.

167

SWEETGUM

Liquidambar styraciflua.
Red Gum.
Beautiful tall tree to heights over 100 feet with a symmetrical pyramidal crown and long straight trunk.

Leaves — Alternate, deciduous, 4-7 inches long, simple but strongly star-shaped with 5-7 leaves and a long slender petiole. Dark glossy green and smooth on the upper surface, paler and essentially hairless below.

Flowers — In spring with the leaves, the sexes separate but on the same tree. Male flowers greenish and inconspicuous in 1 inch drooping, rounded clusters.

Fruit — Maturing in the fall, 1 inch woody balls made up of many little capsules each with 2 sharply pointed beaks and containing tiny winged seeds.

Twigs — Slender, green to reddish brown often with wide corky wings or ridges. The winter buds are up to ½ inch in length covered with glossy scales and cone-shaped with a sharply pointed tip. The pith is large, light brown, and angular instead of round in cross section.

Bark — Corky, light to dark ash gray with pronounced rounded or slightly flattened ridges. The bottoms of the ridges often show a silver streak of light-colored inner bark.

Sweetgum is one of the most common hardwood trees in the East Texas Piney Woods. It is found on frequently flooded river bottoms as well as dry upland hills. These trees are often seen as a pioneer on abandoned fields but they are also members of virgin old-growth forests. The wood is moderately heavy, hard, white with a gray to red brown heartwood with indistinct growth rings and an even grain that takes a satiny finish. These qualities, plus its availability, size, and quick growth rate, make Sweetgum the leading commercial hardwood species in East Texas. (A unique

169

feature is that different types of wood can be cut from the sap and heartwood.) It is used extensively for veneer, furniture, and pulp, but has many other uses as well.

Ornamentally, Sweetgum is one of the most versatile native trees and is widely planted throughout the eastern third of Texas. The fall color is reliably vibrant with shades of yellow, orange, red, and occasionally deep purple. Sweetgums have no serious pests or diseases but are easily damaged by fires, and trees growing in heavy clay soils are weakened by droughts. They are easily transplanted and have a symmetry near perfection when young. One drawback is that the woody thorny fruits or "balls" can be a nuisance, particularly under bare feet or bicycle tires. Sweetgum also has many medicinal qualities, especially effective as an external remedy for wounds and skin problems. Many species of birds feed on the seeds. The name Sweetgum comes from the age-old practice of making chewing gum from the sap. In East Texas, kids often mixed the sap with the shrub Stretchberry (*Forrestiera ligustrina*) fruits, then rolled it into small balls to make bubble gum.

AMERICAN SYCAMORE

Platanus occidentalis.
Buttonwood, Plane Tree.
Large deciduous tree to 100 feet or
more with large spreading branches
forming an irregular crown and a
heavy trunk over three feet in diameter.

Leaves — Alternate, one of the largest simple leaves native to
Texas, up to 1 foot wide, bright green on top, paler and
hairy on the underside, turning brown in autumn. The
leaf stalks are up to 4 inches long and hollow at the base
where they cover the bud.

171

Platanaceae - Sycamore Family

Flowers — The male and female flowers can be found in spring on the same tree but in separate dense round clusters about ½ inch in diameter, borne on short stalks.

Fruit — Brown balls, of small seeds, 1 inch in diameter, ripening in the fall on slender stems 3 to 6 inches in length.

Twigs — Slender, without a true terminal bud, slightly zigzag, buds with three scales or a single caplike scale surrounded by the scar of the leaf base.

Bark — Very distinctive, greenish or cream-color, and sometimes marked with patches of dark green or brown at first, soon flaking off revealing lighter layers of the younger bark. Older trunks are often roughened, fissured, and somewhat blocky, particularly near the base.

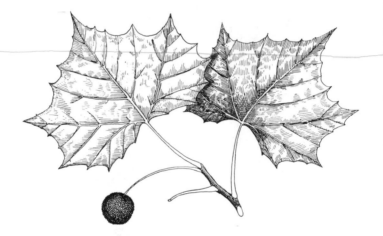

American Sycamore is one of the largest, most easily recognized hardwood trees in Texas. This fast-growing tree is commonly found along streams and rivers, and at the edges of lakes or swamps throughout eastern Texas and west to Zavala County. The wood is whitish with a reddish-brown heartwood. It is moderately heavy and hard with distinct growth rings and prominent rays which give a beautiful figure when quartersawn. Its characteristics of even texture, coarse grain with interlocking fibers, lack of odor and taste, hardness, and resistance to splitting make this the first choice for butchers' meat blocks. Although occasionally

172

used for boxes, crates, and furniture, it tends to warp easily when sawn into lumber and is difficult to work.

Sycamores were once a favored street and shade tree because of their fast growth, low maintenance, and rugged nature; however, their tendency to get sick on poor, dry sites has given them a bad name outside their natural range. They also get quite large planted as a yard tree, often overwhelming a normal-sized residence. Trees under stress are subject to attack by lace bugs and an anthracnose disease which often completely defoliates them before summer. Within their range, however, few trees can rival Sycamore's size, and only the Madrone can compare with the striking contrast of its white bark against a winter's sky.

SMOOTH SYCAMORE. *Platanus occidentalis* var. *glabrata.*

Large tree found along streams and rivers on limestone soils in Central, West, and South Central Texas. It differs from Eastern Sycamore by having few if any secondary teeth besides the main lobings. Some botanists do not recognize this as a separate entity from American Sycamore.

MOUNTAIN MAHOGANY

Cercocarpus montanus.
An evergreen shrub or small tree up to 15 feet with an irregular spreading crown bearing long, feathery-tailed fruit.

Leaves — Oval or obovate, usually toothed at the tip, ¾ to 1¼ inches long, leathery, green to grayish-green above, paler below, usually toothed at the tip, prominent leaf veins on undersurface.

Flowers — White to yellowish, small, borne singly or in clusters of three. Blooms in the spring.

Fruit — Brown, leathery, slender, ¼ inch long, tipped by a whitish plume-like tail one to three inches long.

Twigs — Rigid, brown pubescent when young, often grayish and rough later.

Bark — Gray to brown, smooth, becoming scaly and rough with age.

Mountain Mahogany is an attractive shrub or small tree of the rose family. It grows on dry, rocky uplands in the Trans-Pecos, the western part of the Edwards Plateau, and the Panhandle. It is a slow-growing tree with hard, durable wood. In areas of the Southwest it is called *Palo Duro* (hard stick), while the Navajo name means "stone heavy." The wood has been used for digging sticks and also in making knife handles. Mountain Mahogany does not splinter readily and has been utilized by the Navajo Indians for distaffs in wool spinning, in order to keep the fibers from snagging. The heartwood is dark brown to red, resembling Mahogany, where it derives its common name. The scientific name, *Cercocarpus,* refers to the long-tailed fruit. These whitish, feather-like styles, persisting on the fruit during the summer and fall, serve as gliders or parachutes to disperse the seed. With the aid of a little backlighting from the sun, this silky fruit covering the Mountain Mahogany provides quite a show. The leaves and twigs are considered good browse for cattle, deer, and goats.

When cut down, the Mountain Mahogany will readily sprout from the root. A decoction from its roots has been used to dye wool red. The Tewa Indians of New Mexico drink an infusion of the leaves with salt as a laxative. The attractive foliage and fruit of the tree, as well as its drought tolerance, is reason to consider its use as an ornamental in the Southwest. Mountain Mahogany is quite variable and has three recognized varieties: Var. *glaber* — Leaves without hairs; Var. *argenteus* — Leaves pubescent; Var. *paucidentatus* — Leaves with short, erect hairs; occurring in Brewster, Jeff Davis, and El Paso counties.

175

TEXAS HAWTHORN

Crataegus texana.
Small thorny tree to about 20 feet tall with a densely branched rounded crown and one to several often leaning trunks 6 inches in diameter.

Leaves — Alternate, simple, deciduous, 3-4 inches long. Dull green above, paler and hairy beneath, turning shades of yellow or pink before dropping in the fall.

Flowers — Appearing in mid spring after the leaves have unfolded as few flowered flat-topped clusters, individual flowers about ½ inch across with 5 white petals, numerous stamens showing prominent anthers, an inferior ovary consisting of 1-5 carpels each with its own style.

Fruit — Maturing in the fall, resembling little red apples ½ inch long with a mealy edible flesh containing 1-5 hard bony seeds.

Twigs — Stiff and often armed with straight or slightly curved chestnut brown thorns 1-3 inches long. Twigs often somewhat zigzagged, shiny brown to red brown at first becoming gray with age, showing visible lenticels. Usually with a true terminal bud present, it and the laterals are small glossy, round, scaly, and about the same color as the twig.

Bark — Thin, smooth, and gray at first, becoming red brown or dark gray to almost black with shallow fissures and narrow ridges at maturity.

Texas Hawthorn can be found along creek and river bottoms of the Coastal Plain and into South Central Texas. Hawthorns in general are widely cultivated in the U.S. and abroad for their attractive flowers and the edible fruits which are made into jams, jellies, and wines. They are also utilized for thorny hedges. Many species of birds look to Hawthorns for protected nesting sites in the dense thorny crowns. The small apple-like fruits are consumed by a large number of birds and mammals. Deer also browse the foliage. There are at least 33 species of Hawthorn recognized in Texas; only some of the more common and distinctive ones will be addressed here.

177

PARSLEY HAWTHORN. *Crataegus marshallii.*

Found mostly along fence lines and edges of woods in East Texas. It grows to about 20 feet tall, usually with several trunks, clad in thin gray bark that flakes off revealing a lighter orangish layer underneath. The leaves are from ¾ to 1 ½ inches long borne on a stalk up to 2 inches in length. Parsley Hawthorn fruits are about ⅓ inch long and shiny bright red. They are very high in natural vitamin C and are one of the main ingredients of acerola sold in many health-food stores.

LITTLE-HIP HAWTHORN. *Crataegus spathulata.* Pasture Haw.

Closely resembles Parsley Hawthorn in appearance and range but the leaves are usually not as deeply lobed, and Parsley Hawthorn leaves are rounded, flattened, or heart-shaped at the base whereas Little-Hip leaves taper down along the petiole at the base. The national champion Little-Hip Hawthorn is growing in the Sabine National Forest in Sabine County. It is 33 feet tall, with a crown spread of 30 feet and a trunk circumference of 22 inches.

MAYHAW. *Crataegus opaca.*

Mayhaw is usually restricted to creek and river bottoms in East Texas. It is one of the larger native Hawthorns, reaching 30 feet tall or more with fissured, dark red-brown bark. The leaves are up to 2½ inches long and about half as wide.

Flowers usually appear in early spring, before the leaves, in clusters of 2 – 5 and are about ¾ inch in diameter. This is the Mayhaw that makes such wonderful jellies and jams. The relatively large (up to ¾ inch in diameter) tasty red fruits ripen in May and have always been eagerly sought by country folk. Our state champion Mayhaw can be found in the Angelina National Forest in Angelina County. It is 43 feet tall and has a crown spread of 19 feet and a trunk circumference of 31 inches.

COCKSPUR HAWTHORN. *Crataegus crus-galli.*

A Hawthorn common on dry to fairly moist areas in East, Central, and North Central Texas. It rarely reaches more than 20 feet tall, with gray scaly bark at first, later becoming dark reddish brown and fissured. The shiny leathery leaves are up to 4 inches long but is most readily recognized by its fierce-looking, slightly curved thorns that can be up to 8 inches in length. This is one of our most attractive Hawthorns and is widely cultivated in the eastern part of the state for its glossy foliage, ½-inch-long dull red fruits, abundant half-inch flowers, and formidable thorns.

MOUNTAIN HAWTHORN. *Crataegus tracyi.*

The Mountain Hawthorn is endemic to Texas from Bexar and Comal counties to the Trans-Pecos mountains. It is usually found along creeks and streams but also in some dry and upland situations. In the eastern part of its range it is usually somewhat shrubby but in the Davis Mountains it can become a small tree, 20 feet tall or more, with scaly, gray bark becoming fissured and almost silver black. The flowers appear in mid spring and are followed by ⅓-inch-long mealy fruits which ripen in the fall. This is the most common Hawthorn seen in West Texas.

179

MEXICAN PLUM

Prunus mexicana.
Big Tree Plum.
Large shrub or small solitary tree about 20 feet tall with a 10-inch trunk diameter.

Leaves — Alternate, simple, deciduous, 2 to 4 inches in length, smooth and dark yellow green above, lighter beneath, with prominent netted veins, turning a dirty yellow in the fall.

Flowers — Very early in spring, before or with the leaves, in few flowered clusters of five-petaled white flowers that can be up to 1 inch in diameter and presenting numerous stamens.

180

Fruit — Maturing in midsummer to early fall, rounded about 1 inch in diameter with a thick, juicy edible flesh and a nearly round single seed about ½ inch in length. Mature fruits are a dark purplish red with whitish surface bloom.

Twigs — Slender, somewhat stout, smooth and shiny, light orange brown at first becoming grayish brown with age. Terminal bud to 2 inches in length, pointed and scaly.

Bark — Tight and gray to black when young, becoming scaly, rough, and furrowed with age; very old trees have a brown papery scaly bark.

Mexican Plum is found throughout the eastern half of the state. It usually exists as scattered individuals in the understory of creek bottoms, moist woods, slopes, canyons, and fence rows. The attractive wood is hard, close grained, and takes a good polish but it usually checks badly in drying and is too small for commercial use. The root stocks have been used in grafting because of their relative drought-hardiness and non-suckering habit. Fruits collected wild are not as juicy or prolific as ones from cultivated trees. It was once thought that Indians cultivated these trees but

now the thinking is that orchards arose from seeds acciden-
tally dropped near villages and camps. The juicy fruits are
eaten by only a few species of wildlife — foxes, ring-tailed
cats, and songbirds. The national champion Mexican Plum
is located in Dallas County. It is 60 inches in circumference,
26 feet tall, and covers an area of 35 feet.

FLATWOODS PLUM. *Prunus umbellata.*

This is a large shrub or small tree found in the Piney Woods
of East Texas. It does not sucker to form thickets and can
be distinguished from other native plums by its shorter solitary nature and smaller flowers and leaves — up to 2 inches
long.

CHICKASAW PLUM. *Prunus angustifolia.*

Shrub or small tree that suckers from the roots to form large
colonies. The red or yellow fruits are about ½ inch in diameter and are juicy and edible. The thickets they form are
good for wildlife and this same characteristic makes it good
for erosion control. This plum grows throughout the eastern
and central portions of the state.

WILD-GOOSE PLUM. *Prunus munsoniana.*

Small or large shrub often forming thickets. It is found
mainly from the North to the South Central Texas areas
and can be distinguished from other native plums by its
larger fruits and long narrow leaves that are hairy only
along the veins underneath. Many horticultural varieties
have been developed from this species because of its
relatively large fruits (almost 1 inch in diameter) and fast
growth (can bear fruit at three years of age). Wildlife
also enjoy its protective cover and firm red fruits.

BLACK CHERRY

Prunus serotina.
Wild Cherry.
A medium sized tree, 50 feet or so, but capable of growing to twice that height. In the woods, these trees develop a narrow crown with a slender trunk; in the open, they tend to be broad and rounded with a relatively short trunk.

Leaves — Alternate, simple, deciduous, about 2-5 inches long and 1-2 inches in width with many small blunt-tipped teeth along the margin. They are shiny dark green on top, paler beneath, and turn bright yellow to reddish in the fall. An easy distinguishing feature is the presence of brown tufts near the base of the midrib on the lower leaf surface.

Rosaceae - Rose Family

Flowers — Borne in the spring with the leaves about half grown on drooping narrow cylindrical clusters 4-6 inches long from last year's growth. The pure white flowers are about ¼ inch across with five petals.

Fruit — The pea-sized, single-seeded, juicy dark purple to black fruits ripen in the summer to early fall. They have a bittersweet taste and the calyx persists on the mature fruit.

Twigs — Slender, reddish brown with a white or light brown pith and taste like that of bitter almonds. The buds are sharp pointed and scaly, the terminal bud about ¼ inch long.

Bark — The thin, tight, lighter-colored young bark is a distinctive glossy dark red with many short horizontal lines which are breathing pores (lenticels). The bright green inner bark has a pleasing fragrance but a bitter taste. Older trees develop a black roughened scaly bark with silver flaky tops.

Black Cherry is a relatively fast growing pioneer-type tree commonly found along fence rows, thickets, and the edge of woods. It is the largest native cherry and in some areas the wood is second in value per board foot only to Black Walnut. The hard close-grained wood takes a great polish, seldom warps, is valued for furniture, cabinets, interior trim, handles, and was the preferred wood for printers blocks. The good growth, nice fall color, and the light shade it casts make this a fine landscape tree; however, the thin bark is easily damaged by fire or lawn equipment. It is also subject to attacks from tent caterpillars and black knot fungal galls which can disfigure or kill twigs and branches.

The bittersweet fruits of wild cherry were once very popular for wines, pies, and jellies and as a flavoring. The bark

184

contains toxic properties with the power to calm irritation and dampen nervous excitability, which made it a favorite ingredient in cough medicine. Indian tribes used Black Cherry to treat a variety of things such as hemorrhoids, dysentery, lung problems, and to ease labor pains. Some herbalists still recommend cherries and cherry juice as an intestinal cleanser. The poisonous seeds contain cyanide which is destroyed by cooking. The fruits can be eaten raw but the quality varies from plant to plant. Black Cherry is a very important wildlife food source which often makes the juicy fruit difficult to find. Not only do more than 30 species of birds eat the fruit, but the leaves and twigs are browsed by deer and rabbits. The seeds germinate better after passing through a bird's digestive system; consequently, young cherry trees are frequently found growing under power lines and along fences. Wilted cherry foliage, however, contains cyanic acid and can be poisonous to deer and livestock.

ESCARPMENT CHERRY. *Prunus serotina* subsp. *eximia.*
Black Cherry, Wild Cherry.

Found throughout the Edwards Plateau and South Central Texas area on slopes, canyons, woods, and creek bottoms. The national champion Escarpment Cherry is 64 inches in circumference, and 65 feet tall. It is growing in Lost Maples State Natural Area.

WESTERN CHOKE CHERRY. *Prunus serotina* subsp. *virens.*

This is the Trans-Pecos version of Black Cherry, frequenting mountain canyons and streams, with an isolated population found at the Bexar–Wilson counties line.

COMMON CHOKE CHERRY. *Prunus virginiana.*

This is a small tree, usually less than 30 feet tall, that differs from Black Cherry by having slender instead of rounded teeth on the leaf margins and a deciduous calyx instead of one that persists on the fruit. It is found in East Texas, the Panhandle, and the Trans-Pecos mountain area.

CHERRY LAUREL

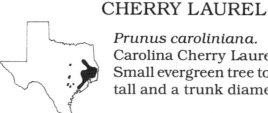

Prunus caroliniana.
Carolina Cherry Laurel.
Small evergreen tree to about 30 feet
tall and a trunk diameter of 1 foot.

Leaves — Alternate, simple, thick, and evergreen, 2-4 inches in
length, shiny dark green above, paler below, smooth margin or with a few sharp teeth, and when crushed have
a strong aroma distinctively like cherry cough drops.
Flowers — In early spring the small white five-petaled fragrant
flowers are borne in dense upright cylindrical clusters
from the leaf axils of last year's growth.

186

Fruit — Black single-seeded ovoids about ½ inch in diameter with a thin bitter flesh, the dry fruit persisting for several months.
Twigs — Slender, smooth, and brownish.
Bark — Thin and smooth but rougher with age, gray to dark green or olive drab.

Carolina Cherry Laurel grows naturally in moist woods and creek bottoms in East Texas west to the Guadalupe River, but is used as an ornamental over much of the eastern half of the state. It is fast growing, somewhat short-lived, fairly disease resistant, easily trained into a hedge, espalier on walls, or can be grown as a handsome evergreen specimen tree which casts a dense shade. For best flowering, only prune or shear after the initial spring display. Cherry Laurel is readily available in most nurseries throughout the eastern half of the state. The seeds and leaves have the same poisonous properties as Black Cherry (*Prunus serotina*) and Common Choke Cherry (*P. virginiana*).

The state champion Carolina Cherry Laurel is 103 inches in trunk circumference, 36 feet tall, and has a crown spread of 41 feet. It is located in Harris County.

TEXAS CRAB APPLE

Pyrus ioensis, Pyrus ioensis var. *texana,* or *Malus ioensis.*
Blanco Crab Apple.
Small tree to about 15 feet tall with a twiggy, open, rounded crown and often a leaning trunk to 10 inches in diameter or a large shrub forming a small thicket by root suckers.

Leaves — Alternate or on spur shoots, simple, deciduous, usually 2-3 inches in length but sometimes longer, margins single- or double-toothed, upper surface green and shiny, the lower surface densely white hairy or occasionally almost smooth, turning yellow or various shades of pink before dropping in the fall.

Flowers — In early spring with the leaves, as few flowered clusters of white or pink, about 1½ inches wide, five petals and a five-lobed calyx, many stamens and one pistil with five styles.

Fruit — Ripening in mid fall as hard green apples up to 2 inches wide and 1 inch thick. The ample, extremely tart flesh encloses 1 to (rarely) 3 black seeds about ¼ inch long.

Twigs — Slender or stout, reddish brown with spine-tipped spur shoots, densely woolly at first, becoming smooth with age. Terminal bud present, reddish brown, rounded with 3-6 scales.

Bark — Thin, gray brown, and tight when young, becoming dark steel gray and scaly and finally turning darker and developing shallow vertical fissures and longitudinal ridges about ¼ inch thick.

Texas Crab Apple represents the southwestern extent of the Wild Crab Apple's range. In Texas, its natural occurrence is restricted to stream banks and the heads of canyons in Blanco, Kerr, and Kendall counties. The tart fruits are barely edible raw but are great for jellies. Wildlife enjoy the small apples but the trees are not abundant enough to become an important food source. The Texas Crab Apple is rare and somewhat threatened in the wild, but some nurseries are beginning to offer them for their beautiful spring floral display and their tart fruit.

WILD CRAB APPLE. *Pyrus angustifolia.*
Southern Crab Apple.

A small tree about 15 feet tall, uncommon in Texas, found in creek bottoms, thickets, and woods in the southeast portion of the state. It differs from Texas Crab Apple in its eastern range and having leaves that are hairless at maturity.

LOQUAT

Eriobotrya japonica.

Small evergreen tree to about 20 feet tall with a rounded crown; one to several trunks eight inches in diameter.

Leaves — Alternate, simple, usually clustered near the branch tips, thick and evergreen, 6 to 10 inches in length, bright green and shiny on top, reddish hairy below.

Flowers — Blooming in early to midwinter, in branched terminal clusters up to 7 inches long, individual flowers very fragrant, roughly ½ inch wide and densely covered with reddish brown hairs, 5 petals, sepals, and numerous stamens.

Fruit — Maturing in the spring, yellow, somewhat pear-shaped, up to 1½ inches long with a fairly thick tasty flesh surrounding several large, dark brown seeds.

Twigs — Stout, densely covered with gray or whitish hairs when young, becoming smooth as they get older.

Bark — Thin and smooth, tan or light brown at first and eventually peeling off revealing an orangish underlayer.

190

Loquat is originally a native of southwestern China but was introduced into Western cultivation from Japan, hence the species name. It is a popular ornamental tree planted in the eastern half of the state. Since it blooms so late in the year the flowers are frequently frozen before they can develop fruits. Therefore they only reseed and establish themselves with any consistency south of a line through about the Austin area. It is not an aggressive tree so individuals that naturalize outside of cultivation are most often found in urban settings where their parents were planted as landscape specimens.

As an ornamental, Loquat has many favorable qualities. They tolerate alkaline soils, grow reasonably fast, and are fairly drought resistant once established. The large coarse foliage lends a semitropical look to any landscape and the flowers are extremely fragrant. Fire blight has been known to plague some trees but otherwise they are relatively free of serious pests and diseases. When the flowers appear they are swarmed by bees as the weather permits and the subsequent fruit tastes somewhat like a cross between a peach and an apricot. It can be eaten raw or made into delicious jellies or wine. In the early 1900's Loquat was grown in southern California for commerical fruit production but is not as popular today and few of these plantations are in operation. In China, Loquat is valued medicinally for its respiratory healing properties. It is known as "dew drop" in Chinese because of a refreshing tea made from its leaves.

This is a fine ornamental semitropical tree that receives little fanfare but continues to be a constant in the nursery trade, valued for its bold foliage, lack of serious problems, and ability to fit well in small spaces.

CHINESE TALLOW TREE

Sapium sebiferum.

Medium sized tree 30 feet or more tall with a spreading rounded or tapered crown and a short, often twisted or fluted, trunk 12-18 inches in diameter.

Leaves — Alternate, simple, deciduous, resembling poplar leaves somewhat, 1½ to 3 inches long, slightly wider than long, smooth on both surfaces, yellow to dark green turning red, yellow, orange, or purple in the fall.

Flowers — Appearing in late spring to early summer, male and female flowers together in drooping tassel-like clusters 1½ to over 3 inches long, golden yellow. The female parts are near the base of the cluster and the male flowers display their showy anthers for the remainder of the spike.

Fruit — Ripening in the fall, as hard round or three-lobed capsules often with a whitish bloom like blueberries, about ½ inch thick usually made up of 3 separate chambers each containing a single wax-covered seed about ⅜ inch long, often persisting on the tree through the winter.

Twigs — Thin and weak green at first, becoming gray brown covered with small lenticels. Winter twigs often have an inch or more of terminal dieback due to cold damage.

Bark — Gray brown to dark brown with flat ridges and shallow fissures often marked with lighter splotches caused by lichens.

Chinese Tallow is, as its name implies, a native of China. It has been widely cultivated in the Gulf Coast States and become naturalized, even pestiferous, in some areas. In Southeast Texas, Tallow tree quickly covers untended fields choking out other vegetation. It was originally brought in and is still planted for its fast growth rate, adaptability, lack of pests and diseases, and outstanding fall color. An oil may be pressed from the seed, and in the past "vegetable tallow" was obtained from the waxy coating and used in the making of Chinese soaps, candles, and as a cloth dressing. A black dye can be made from the leaves, and the sap is considered poisonous. Mexican Jumping Beans are a species of *Sapium* native to Southwest Arizona and northern Mexico. The seeds actually move as a result of a moth larvae which eats out the inside of the "bean." This tree has very little to offer wildlife, and for some unknown reason bird nests are rarely seen in them. The national champion Chinese Tallow, located in Travis County, is 52 feet tall, and has a crown spread of 86 feet and a trunk circumference of 120 inches.

TITI

Cyrilla racemiflora.
Swamp Cyrilla.
Tall shrub or small tree often forming dense thickets.

Leaves — Alternate, simple, usually persisting through the winter to drop the following season, 2 to 3 inches long and about ⅓ as wide.

Flowers — Appearing in mid spring, as many tiny white blossoms about ⅛ inch across, with 5 stamens, petals, sepals, and a single pistil. The flowers are densely crowded on elongated narrowly cylindrical clusters about 4 to 6 inches long found in groups near the branch tips.

Fruit — Ripening in early fall as tiny somewhat egg-shaped capsules persisting through the winter, about ⅛ inch long and containing one to several minute hard seeds.

Twigs — Slender, round or somewhat 3-angled, shiny brown or gray, smooth with a dark brown terminal bud up to ¼ inch long with several overlapping scales.

194

Bark — Thin, reddish brown and shiny when young, turning gray and separating into thin shreddy scales as the tree gets older.

Titi is found in Southeast Texas in low wet areas, along streams and riverbanks. It is usually frowned on by foresters because of the dense almost impenetrable thickets the tree sometimes forms but it does have some ornamental qualities in cultivation. The shiny, dark green, almost evergreen leaves that turn red before they drop and the prolific white blossoms make it a handsome tree in its own right. It is not a particularly versatile plant but does best in moist locations with a little shade. Early settlers used the bark scraped from the trunk near the soil level as an astringent to stop bleeding wounds. This tree has its most favorable reputation as being one of the last and most prolific of the spring honey plants to bloom. Bees diligently work the flowers making an excellent table honey with a dark reddish-amber color and a mild flavor.

195

AMERICAN HOLLY

Ilex opaca.
Small evergreen tree to about 40 feet tall with a narrow pyramid-shaped crown of short spreading branches and a short, straight trunk about 1 foot in diameter.

Leaves — Alternate, simple, evergreen. Somewhat stiff and leathery, the margin varying from almost entire to remotely spiny-toothed. About 2-4 inches long and half as wide, dull green above, paler below, persisting for up to three years.

Flowers — In late spring to early summer, the sexes on separate trees, flowers somewhat fragrant, small and greenish with 5 petals. The male flowers in clusters of 3-10 arising from the axils of young leaves. Female flowers similar but solitary or in clusters of 2-3.

Fruit — Maturing in fall but persisting through the winter. Red (rarely yellow), rounded, mealy berry about ⅓ to ½ inch in diameter borne on a short stalk and containing 4 grooved seeds.

Twigs — Slender to somewhat stout with rounded winter buds up to ⅓ inch in length.

Bark — Relatively thin, light gray, with small warty roughenings. Patches of algae often create splotches of yellow, green, or red on older trunks.

American Holly is a slow growing, long-lived, usually understory tree found along stream banks, upper river bottoms, and moist woods in East Texas west to Wilson County. It is one of our most familiar trees, easily recognized, especially in winter, by the narrow bushy triangular crown and

197

persistent red berries on female trees. The red winter fruits and thick evergreen leaves have made this holly a favorite for Christmas decorations. American Holly is a very good ornamental from which many cultivars have been developed. It is somewhat difficult to transplant from the wild, and both sexes need to be present for good berry production.

The brightly colored berries and handsome foliage also make a useful tree for attracting wildlife. Many species of songbirds, including old favorites such as robins, bluebirds, and mockingbirds, find food and winter shelter in the branches of American Holly. Holly wood is one of the unique American hardwoods, being almost ivory white when first cut but gradually turning brown when exposed to the air. It was formerly valuable for such things a piano keys and cabinet inlays. Although the berries are a popular Christmas decoration, they contain a poisonous substance that can cause diarrhea and vomiting. American Holly is the state tree of Delaware.

YAUPON HOLLY. *Ilex vomitoria.*

A small branchy tree usually having several trunks up to about 25 feet tall. The glossy evergreen leaves have small rounded teeth instead of spines and are about ½ to two inches in length and half as wide. It is usually found grow-

ing naturally in Southeast Texas westward through Central Texas, also common along the eastern margin of the Edwards Plateau west to the Frio River and to Matagorda Bay on sandy pinelands, along streams, and in some drier areas. Sometimes Yaupons sucker from roots to form dense thickets of stiff branches. Yaupons have become increasingly popular as a landscape plant. The shiny dark green foliage contrasting with the light-colored bark and the added attraction of the bright red fruits persisting over winter make this plant very popular. It also has the ability to grow under many different conditions of soil, dry or moist situations, sun or shade.

Several dwarf varieties have been developed as well as weeping and yellow-berried cultivars. Birds are fond of the scarlet fruits and enjoy the protection of the stiff branches and evergreen leaves. The leaves contain a small amount of caffeine, and a coffee substitute can be made by steeping the dried leaves in hot water. Indians made a beverage called the "Black Drink" which they used for a ritualistic purging ceremony—hence the species name *vomitoria*. Like other hollies, Yaupon berries contain a poisonous substance that can cause vomiting and diarrhea. The national champion Yaupon is 32 feet tall and has a trunk circumference of 46 inches and a crown spread of 37 feet. It is located at Devers in Liberty County.

POSSUMHAW. *Ilex decidua.*
Deciduous Holly, Deciduous Yaupon.

A shrub or small tree that grows in East and Central Texas usually along creeks, streams, or fence lines. Unlike the previous species, this one has deciduous leaves 1¼ to 3 inches in length which appear in clusters at the end of short spur branches. When the foliage drops in the fall, female plants brightly display their ⅓-inch orange-red fruits which are enjoyed by many species of wildlife including bobwhite quail and mockingbirds. Female plants have become more commonly used in landscape plantings under the name of Deciduous Yaupon.

CAROLINA HOLLY. *Ilex ambigua.*

A deciduous holly found in moist woods in East Texas that occasionally reaches small tree stature. The thin leaves are sharply serrated on the margins but not spine tipped. They are about 1 ½ to 3 inches in length and broadest at or below the middle, whereas Possumhaw Holly leaves are widest at or above the middle. Carolina Holly leaves are also pointed at the tip while Possumhaw leaves are usually somewhat rounded.

WINTERBERRY. *Ilex verticillata.*
Black Alder.

A small deciduous tree to about 15 feet tall with persistent red berries throughout midwinter. Differs from other native hollies by having large (up to 5 inches long), deciduous leaves, and flowers usually with more than 5 petals and calyx lobes. In Texas it is restricted to wet areas in the southeast portion of the state but is more common in the southeastern states.

MOUNTAIN WINTERBERRY. *Ilex montana.*

Usually a shrub or small tree found on sandy soils of deep East Texas. It is distinguished from other deciduous hollies by having petals and calyx lobes with hairy margins, long pointed leaves, and grooved seeds, whereas Winterberry has leaves with rounded, toothed margins and smooth seeds.

BLUEWOOD CONDALIA

Condalia hookeri.
Brazil, Capul Negro.
A shrub or small tree with an irregular spreading crown, often forming thickets.

Leaves — Bright green and glossy. ½ to ¼ inches long, rounded at the tip, tapering toward the base, sometimes notched or with a single tooth at the tip.

Flowers — Small and inconspicuous, greenish, two or more clustered in the junction of the leaves.

Fruit — Rounded, dark blue to black, fleshy, very sweet, containing a single flattened seed.

Twigs — Green and velvety when young, becoming smooth and brown or gray later. Branches ending in sharp thorns.

Bark — Thin, smooth when young, becoming furrowed with age. Brown to light gray.

201

This shrub or small tree is found growing in dryer soils of the Hill Country, West Texas, and most abundantly in South Texas. Bluewood Condalia is a spiny plant often forming thickets. Occasionally it will reach heights up to 30 feet. The wood is hard, heavy, dense, and red in color. It has little value other than firewood. The wood reportedly yields a blue dye but recent attempts by the San Antonio Botanical Center staff only extracted a light red or pink color.

The tree flowers in the spring and fruits sporadically during the summer. The dark blue fruit is quite sweet and edible, making good jelly and wine. It is often a challenge finding enough ripe fruit at one time, however. Many types of wildlife also find the fruit attractive, including birds, squirrels, raccoons, and opossum. The national champion is found at Santa Ana National Wildlife Refuge near Alamo. It stands 32 feet tall with a 54-inch circumference. Although not as large, another nice specimen grows in the courtyard of San José Mission of San Antonio, in the northwest corner near the granary.

CAROLINA BUCKTHORN

Rhamnus caroliniana.
Indian Cherry.
Large shrub or small tree 25 feet tall
with an upright oval crown and a
slender trunk six inches in diameter.

Leaves — Alternate, simple, late deciduous, somewhat leathery, shiny dark green and smooth above, slightly hairy or
smooth and paler below, 2-6 inches long, with 8-10 pairs
of distinctive lateral veins running parallel to the margins, turning various shades of pink to orange before
dropping in midwinter.
Flowers — In late spring or early summer, greenish white, borne
on tiny stalks, singly or in small clusters from the leaf axils,
about ⅛ inch wide, perfect with 5 petals, sepals, and
stamens.
Fruit — Maturing late summer or early fall on short stalks as
pea-sized fleshy berries turning pink, red, and finally to
black as they mature, containing 3-4 hard seeds.

Twigs — Slender, red brown at first, becoming gray later with a round, whitish continuous pith, terminal bud naked, about ¼ inch long, brown woolly, side buds rounded and smaller.

Bark — Thin and tight, smooth or with faint furrows, becoming gray and often marked with darker blotches.

Carolina Buckthorn is found throughout the eastern half of the state west through the Edwards Plateau. In East Texas it is most often an understory tree associated with moist woods. Farther west it is frequently found along fence lines, creeks, at the heads of draws, and in brush associated with canyon rims. The young wood is a distinctive bright yellow color. Birds love the abundant berries and often strip the branches clean. This is an attractive and versatile native ornamental, adapted to a wide range of sites and tolerant of sun or shade. It has handsome foliage, good fall color, and reliably abundant and showy fruits borne over a relatively long period. Most plants look better if they are cut back periodically to keep them from getting leggy. The bark of a western relative provides the cascara laxative drug of commerce. The state champion Carolina Buckthorn is 33 feet tall, has a trunk girth of 13 inches, and covers an area of 24 feet. It is part of the Sabine National Forest in Sabine County.

BIRCH-LEAF BUCKTHORN. *Rhamnus betulaefolia.*

A large shrub or, rarely, a small tree found at higher elevations in moist canyons of the Trans-Pecos mountains. It differs from *R. caroliniana* by having leaves with densely hairy undersides.

204

CAROLINA BASSWOOD

Tilia caroliniana.
Large tree 75 feet tall with a narrow irregular rounded crown and a 2-foot diameter trunk that is often some-what leaning. Wild trees occasionally have several smaller trunks suckering from near the base of the largest stem.

Leaves — Alternate, simple, deciduous, vaguely heart-shaped but with a lopsided or flattened base, long pointed tip, and coarsely-toothed margins, smooth and dark shiny green above, paler and somewhat hairy beneath.

205

Flowers — In late spring to early summer, fragrant white five-petaled flowers almost ½ inch across in clusters of 8 to 15 that dangle from a leaflike bract 4 to 5 inches in length.

Fruit — Maturing in fall as round, pea-sized, downy gray brown, almost woody fruits enclosing one or two hard seeds hanging from the peculiar leafy bract as do the flowers.

Twigs — Slender, greenish-red to red, with a clear sap, no true terminal bud, and winter buds that are red or red and green having only two to four overlapping bud scales giving them a slightly lopsided appearance.

Bark — Gray to dark gray or gray-brown, smooth on young trunks especially suckers but older main trunks developing interlacing flat-topped ridges, separated by coarse furrows.

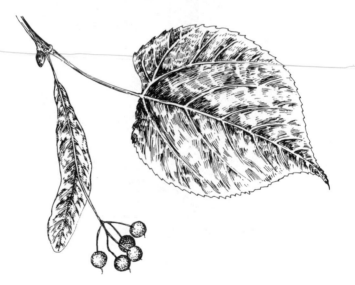

Carolina Basswood is found along streams, valleys, and creek bottoms in East and Central Texas. These trees usually exist as scattered individuals in the forest and are most common on fertile soils. Basswood is sometimes confused with Red Mulberry but can be distinguished from that species by having lopsided leaf bases, peculiar fruits, and the winter buds usually have only 2 to 4 scales whereas Mulberry buds typically have at least 5 scales.

The name Basswood comes from the bast or fiber obtained from the bark of these trees. Indians and early settlers made cordage by soaking or simmering the bark to remove the fibers. The wood was formerly important for many specialty uses. It has a whitish sapwood, merging gradually into a pale brown heartwood. In general it is light, straight grained, soft, odorless, and tasteless with fairly distinct growth rings. It was most commonly used for furniture core stock because it does not warp or check readily. Some of the more specialized uses were frames for bee honeycombs, artist's charcoal, and piano keys. The straight even grain makes it one of the best native woods for carving or whittling.

Basswood flowers make an excellent white-colored honey and have been used in a nerve-soothing tea. The flowers and leaves have long been used to treat colds, coughs, and sore throats. Minor burns and skin irritations were treated by using the mucilaginous inner bark. The winter leaf buds can be picked and eaten fresh off the twig. As an ornamental, Basswood is attractive and relatively free from problems but it is hard to find in the nursery trade. The national champion Carolina Basswood is 92 feet tall and has a trunk circumference of 110 inches and a crown spread of 50 feet. It is located near Leakey in Real County. The different species of Basswood are notoriously difficult to separate. There are two other species of *Tilia* that occur naturally in Texas.

AMERICAN BASSWOOD. *Tilia americana.* American Linden.

Medium to large sized tree found in Northeast Texas. It is distinguished by the leaves and twigs being virtually hairless.

FLORIDA BASSWOOD. *Tilia floridana.*

Medium sized tree found in East and Central Texas. Distinguished from other Basswoods by having hairy young leaves that become smooth with maturity.

BLACK TUPELO

Nyssa sylvatica.
Black Gum, Sour Gum.
Tree to 100 feet tall with short, crooked branches coming off the trunk at right angles, forming a narrow oblong crown with a flattened top. The straight trunk is usually unbranched nearly to the top with a diameter of 2-3 feet.

Leaves — Alternate, simple, deciduous, 2-5 inches in length, glossy, dark green above with distinct veins that are somewhat parallel, paler beneath. The margin is smooth and a little thicker than the rest of the leaf which turns brilliant red to burgundy in the fall.

208

Flowers — In mid to late spring with the leaves, the sexes sometimes on separate trees or the flowers perfect, greenish,
inconspicuous, five-parted; female flowers in two to
several flowered clusters, male flowers in dense many-
flowered heads borne on slender stalks.
Fruit — Maturing in the fall, oval, ½ inch long, blue-black; thin,
sour-fleshed drupe enclosing a single ribbed seed.
Twigs — Slender, reddish brown, slightly hairy at first but becoming smooth later, with dark brown teardrop-shaped
buds standing out from the twig. The pith is chambered
and the twig as a whole is difficult to break off a branch
with bare hands.
Bark — Reddish brown to gray or black, moderately thick and
becoming broken into conspicuous separate blocks.

Black Tupelo is found growing in moist woods, river bottoms, and open woods on sandy soils in the East Texas Timber Belt. It is usually found as scattered individuals that
are easily recognized from a distance by their craggy
branches and early red fall color. The name Tupelo comes
from an Indian name for the tree. Most large Black Tupelos
have a hollow trunk because the wood rots unusually fast
for a bottomland tree. This makes it a valuable haven or
"den tree" for many species of forest wildlife. The hollow
trunks were once cut into sections and covered with boards
to create bee hives, and the excellent Tupelo Honey made
from the flowers is well known where the tree grows wild.

The wood of Black Tupelo is white to grayish with indistinct growth rings. It is moderately heavy and hard with

209

a tough interlocking grain that makes it very difficult to split. The wood was generally considered of little commercial value but has found use as pressure-treated railroad ties, mallet heads, shipping crates, and berry boxes. Many species of wildlife feed on Black Tupelo fruits. The tree is a beautiful ornamental but is somewhat difficult to transplant from the wild. It has few disease problems but is readily scarred or killed by fire. The national champion Black Tupelo is 139 feet tall and has a trunk circumference of 181 inches and a crown spread of 83 feet. It is located in Robertson County.

WATER TUPELO. *Nyssa aquatica.*
Water Gum.

Large tree to about 100 feet tall with a narrow oblong crown and a long straight trunk a few feet in diameter, often strongly flared at the base. This is a true swamp species that is usually found within a few feet of the water level in the backwaters of East Texas rivers and swamps. It is distinguished from Black Tupelo by the large, long-pointed leaves, 5-10 inches long, stout twigs, the often flared base, and the large fruit about 1 inch in length. The wood is more resistant to rotting and the trunk is straight and free of low branches; consequently it is used more commercially than its cousin but generally for the same purposes. The flowers are as good a bee food as its less aquatic relative. Many species of wildlife eat the fruits, which are usually borne in heavy seed crops every year. Water Tupelo is often the dominant swamp tree replacing heavily cut Bald Cypress stands.

TEXAS MADRONE

Arbutus xalapensis.
Naked Indian, Lady's Legs, Madroña, Manzanita.

An evergreen tree or shrub up to 30 feet with stout crooked branches distinguished by its reddish peeling bark.

Leaves — Evergreen, ovate to oblong, pointed to rounded at the tip, alternate, 1 to 4 inches long. Dark green above, paler and sometimes pubescent beneath. Petiole green to reddish.

Flowers — White or pinkish, small, urn-shaped, found in terminal clusters about 4 inches long. Blooms appear from about February to April.

Fruit — Round, ¼ to ⅓ inch in diameter, red to orange, fleshy, edible, appear October to December.

Bark — Thin, pink to reddish brown, peeling away to expose the white to reddish inner bark.

211

Ericaceae - Heath Family

The Madrone is one of the more beautiful trees of Texas. The thin pinkish-to-red exfoliating bark reveals a smooth tan to reddish inner bark which the common names Naked Indian and Lady's Legs so appropriately describe. This tree is found on limestone or igneous hills in localized areas of the Edwards Plateau, the Trans-Pecos, and the southern High Plains. It also occurs in southeastern New Mexico and

south into Mexico and Guatemala. The Madrone flowers are creamy white to pinkish, in clusters, followed by round fleshy red to orange fruit. The fruit is sweet and readily eaten by birds and other wildlife. The name Madrone is derived from the Spanish word *madroño,* meaning strawberry tree. Father Juan Crespi of the Spanish Portolá expedition in California in the 1760's noticed the similarity of the Pacific Madrone to the Strawberry Tree *(Arbutus unedo)* of Spain. This close relative from the Mediterranean has larger fruit. Our Texas Madrone is occasionally called Manzanita, meaning "little apple," because of its red fruit.

The wood of Texas Madrone is hard, coarse grained, and reddish brown. It has been used to make tool handles, and charcoal, as well as for fuel. The bark and roots were used as a source of yellow, orange, and brown dyes. The leaves are said to have astringent and diuretic properties. They are often browsed by deer, goats, and to a lesser extent by cattle. The Madrone seems to be on the decline for in some areas of its range very few seedlings are seen. This could be attributed to grazing pressure and a lack of consistent moisture. The broken range of the Madrone in Texas may reflect its much wider distribution during the cool, moist climate of the Ice Age. Often the only seedlings able to sur-

212

vive are those that germinate under the protection of a juniper or other "nurse tree."

Because of its attractiveness, the Texas Madrone certainly has ornamental potential. It is generally considered to be a difficult plant to grow. The seedlings are susceptible to a fungus at about 3 to 4 inches tall. The Madrone also lacks root hairs, which can be hard on a young plant if it dries out. Growing Madrones from seed is kind of like "witching" for water. People either can do it or they can't. Those who grow them successfully claim it's easy and that there should be more plants available commercially. Recent studies have indicated that Madrones have a mycorrhizal relationship with a root/soil fungus which benefits both the tree and the fungus. This fungus enables the plant to absorb minerals more efficiently, and the fungus, in turn, is believed to benefit by obtaining nutrients from the root. Although this occurs in other members of the Heath family, it has not been irrevocably proven on the Madrone. In any case, this is truly a beautiful tree worthy of recognition. One can find the national champion Texas Madrone at Big Bend National Park. It has a height of 32 feet, a circumference of 112 inches, and a crown spread of 42 feet.

FARKLEBERRY. *Vaccinium arboreum.*
Sparkleberry.

Irregular shrub or small tree to about 25 feet tall with shiny, smooth, dark green leaves about ½ inch in length. The small, drooping white urn-shaped flowers appear in spring, followed by round, black, inedible berries about ¼ inch wide maturing in the fall. It is commonly found on sandy soils throughout East Texas west to the Bastrop area and Nueces County.

213

GUM BUMELIA

Bumelia lanuginosa.
Woolly Buckthorn, Gum Elastic, Chittamwood.
Small tree occasionally more than 40 feet high with stiff, spiny branches forming a narrow rounded crown and a slender straight trunk about 1 foot in diameter.

Leaves — Alternate, simple, nearly evergreen in mild winters, 1 to 4 inches in length, often clustered on short spur branches, dark green and shiny above, rusty brown or white hairy on the underside.

Flowers — In early to midsummer as inconspicuous, five-petaled white flowers, somewhat fragrant, to about $1/5$ inch long, borne in small clusters from the leaf axils.

Fruit — Ripening in the fall, oval, up to 1 inch in length, somewhat fleshy, black, off a slender stalk, with a single brown seed up to ½ inch long.

Twigs — Slender but rigid, rounded in cross section, often armed with stout thorn-tipped branchlets, covered with red brown or gray white hairs but soon becoming smooth.

Bark — Relatively thick, brown tinged with red, soon develop-

214

ing into a distinctive pattern of deep fissures and narrow interlacing flat-topped ridges. Middle aged trunks and branches often have curved flakes arising from the ridges.

Gum Bumelia and its several varieties are usually found on dry rocky soils along fence lines or in open woods, but it attains its greatest size near the edges of creek bottoms in East, Central, and parts of West Texas. The wood is yellowish with a brown heartwood. It is hard, close grained, has an attractive figure, and takes a good polish, but it is usually only large enough for small specialty items or cabinet wood. Children used to chew the gum that exuded from the bark and called it "chicady." Kiowa and Comanche Indians allegedly were fond of the fruits which most people today regard as unpalatable. Birds rarely let a ripe fruit fall from the tree.

Bumelia would make an interesting ornamental but newly transplanted trees are often done in by borers. The common name Chittamwood is in reference to a Biblical tree, the Shittamwood, and has been given rather loosely to several other tree species. The Biblical Ark of the Covenant was made of Chittamwood. Our national champion Gum Bumelia is 80 feet tall and has a trunk circumference of 83 inches and a crown spread of 66 feet. It is growing in Robertson County.

COMA. *Bumelia celastrina.*
La Coma.

Small tree to about 20 feet tall but often only a thorny shrub found on the South Texas Plains. It differs from other Bumelia by having 1 to 1½-inch-long evergreen leaves that are usually hairless on the lower surface.

BUCKTHORN BUMELIA. *Bumelia lycioides.*

A shrub or small tree up to 25 feet with narrow, pointed leaves and stout spines. It is rather uncommon in East Texas.

SNOWDROP TREE

Halesia diptera.
Two-Wing Silver Bell.
Small tree about 30 feet tall with an irregular rounded crown of ascending branches and a slender trunk 10 inches in diameter.

Leaves — Alternate, simple, deciduous, 2-5 inches long, 1½ to 4 inches wide, hairy at first but becoming smooth with age. Turning yellow before dropping in the fall.

Flowers — In the spring after the leaves have unfolded, hanging four-petaled, bell-shaped white, about 1 inch long, in clusters of 3-6, with 8 or more stamens.

Fruit — Maturing in late summer, 1-2 inches long, hanging, oblong, with 2 corky or papery wings enclosing a single spindle-shaped seed.

Twigs — Slender and round in cross section, slightly zigzag, reddish brown, hairless but the bark often peeling into thin papery strips on older twigs, buds about ⅛ inch long, sometimes on short stalks, the pith chambered.

Bark — Thin, reddish brown, smooth at first, becoming somewhat scaly at maturity.

Snowdrop Tree is an attractive understory tree found in
moist woods throughout the southern half of the East Texas
Piney Woods. It is a handsome fast growing ornamental
with very few insect or disease problems. The flowers attract hummingbirds and it will tolerate sun or shade but
blooms best with more sun.

CAROLINA SILVER BELL. *Halesia caroliniana.*

A small tree to about 30 feet tall found as uncommon understory individuals in the East Texas Piney Woods. It differs
from Snowdrop Tree by having larger leaves up to 7 inches

long and four-winged fruits. This is a beautiful ornamental that rivals Flowering Dogwood for its spring floral display.

AMERICAN SNOW BELL. *Styrax americana.*
Silver Bells.

Shrub or small tree to about 10 feet tall found throughout East Texas in moist woods or river bottoms. It differs from the Halesias by having a continuous pith, smaller flowers, and round, pea-sized fruits. The national champion American Snowbell is located in the Sabine National Forest. It stands 13 feet tall and has a trunk girth of 8 inches and a crown spread of 15 feet.

EASTERN PERSIMMON

Diospyros virginiana.
Common Persimmon.
Medium sized tree to about 40 feet tall with spreading, often crooked, drooping branches forming a cylindrical round-topped crown and a trunk 2 feet in diameter.

Leaves — Alternate, simple, deciduous with a smooth margin, 3-6 inches long, shiny dark green above, paler and somewhat hairy below, thickish, turning pink to yellow in the fall.

Flowers — In late spring or early summer, the sexes on separate trees, ½ to ¾ inches in length, urn-shaped, yellow green with 4 petals and 4 sepals, the male flowers in clusters of 2 or 3 from the leaf axils, females usually single and borne on a short stalk.

Fruit — Maturing in fall or early winter, rounded with a thick edible flesh topped by the dry, papery persistent four-lobed calyx, 1 to 2½ inches in diameter, orange to purple, with 8 flattened reddish-brown seeds about ½ inch in length.

Twigs — Slender, gray to reddish brown, with a false terminal bud giving them a slight zigzag appearance, buds reddish about ⅓ inch in length with greatly overlapping scales, pith continuous or diaphragmmed in the same twigs.

Bark — Dark brown turning blackish and deeply divided into many distinctive small, square, thick, scaly blocks or plates.

Eastern Persimmon is found on a variety of sites from river bottoms to dry upland fence rows where it forms dense thickets from root sprouts. It is found mainly in the eastern third of Texas but scattered populations exist as far west as Bexar and Kendall counties. This is a famous tree that was well known to the Indians and early settlers. Unripened or green Persimmon fruit seems more astringent than full strength alum and is generally considered edible only after the first frost. The ripe pulp is delicious and is regularly prepared in a variety of ways such as puddings, cakes, and preserves. Indians made a bread from the pulp and the seeds were sometimes used as a coffee substitute during the Civil War.

Persimmon wood is noted for its toughness, strength, hardness, and ability to absorb shock; it becomes smoother with wear. Its primary uses were for textile weaving shuttles, billiard cues, spools, bobbins, and golf-club heads. Many species of wildlife eat the fruit and during the winter one can find clusters of these seeds where the rest of an animal's droppings have worn away. The habit of suckering from the roots on poorer sites makes Eastern Persimmon valuable for erosion control and land reclamation. Ornamentally, the trees are attractive for their crooked appearance and interesting bark, but they don't often give much of a fall show because the leaves tend to turn colors individually instead of all at once. They have a deep taproot and are fairly difficult to transplant. Female trees often drop plenty of fleshy fruits that can make a mess when squashed. Therefore they should not be planted near walkways, patios, driveways, or swimming pools. The national champion Common Persimmon is 60 feet tall and has a trunk circumference of 146 inches and a crown spread of 58 feet. It is growing in Leon County.

TEXAS PERSIMMON

Diospyros texana.
Mexican Persimmon, Chapote Negro.
A shrub or small tree up to 35 feet
with a rounded crown and smooth
gray bark.

Leaves — Oval to oblong, 1-2 inches long, leathery, often fuzzy
beneath, leaf edges slightly rolled under.
Flowers — ½ inch long, greenish white, somewhat bell-shaped
with 4 lobes, male and female flowers on separate plants.
Fruit — Round and plump, ¾ to 1 inch across, black when ripe,
sweet, edible pulp.
Twigs — Very small, slightly fuzzy.
Bark — Gray, smooth, with thin layers peeling off revealing the
lighter-colored inner bark.

The Texas Persimmon is found in dry rocky areas of Central, South, and West Texas, and infrequently seen near the coast. It is also native to northern Mexico and thus sometimes called Mexican Persimmon. This shrub or tree, which is related to the Eastern Persimmon, is readily distinguished by its smooth gray bark and small leathery leaves.

223

The fruit of the Texas Persimmon is black when ripe. It is sweet and edible and stains easily. In Mexico, the fruit is used to dye animal hides. Birds and mammals— particularly javelina—are fond of the fruit. The Persimmon leaves are browsed by deer and goats.

Texas Persimmon is a relative of the Ebony of Asia, known for its durable black wood used for fine furniture and piano keys. The wood of Texas Persimmon is very heavy with black

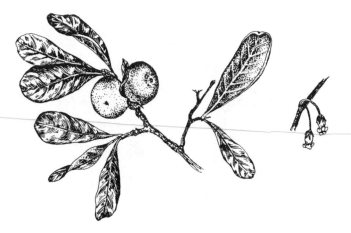

heartwood and a bright yellow sapwood. It is used in making tool handles and for lathe products. The wood is reported to be ideal for saltshakers as it absorbs moisture readily. On shallow rocky hillsides of the Edwards Plateau, the Texas Persimmon can take on a shrubby form which will spread and become an invasive pest. In the proper site, however, this tree is very attractive and worthy of cultivation. There is a small population of Texas Persimmon plants in the Lower Rio Grande Valley with yellow fruit which are locally called *Chapote Amarillo*. The national champion Texas Persimmon is 26 feet tall, with a trunk circumference of 67 inches, and shades an area 31 feet across. It is located in Uvalde County.

SWEET LEAF

Symplocos tinctoria.
Horse Sugar.
Semi-evergreen tree to about 30 feet tall with a wide, loose crown and a straight or slightly leaning trunk reaching 1 foot in diameter.

Leaves — Alternate, simple, persisting late into the winter but eventually falling. Glossy dark green above, slightly hairy or pale beneath, up to 6 inches long and 2 inches wide, turning yellow or red before dropping, with a faint sweet taste when chewed. Often hanging loosely on the tree giving it a wilted appearance.
Flowers — In late winter or early spring, hugging the naked older wood as fragrant yellow clusters up to 2½ inches

225

across made up of 2 to 10 flowers with 5 small sepals, petals, and numerous showy exerted stamens.

Fruit — Ripening in late summer to early fall, orange brown, somewhat oval about ½ inch long crowned by the remains of the persistent 5 sepals.

Twigs — Moderately stout, greenish at first, turning gray brown with age, somewhat hairy, with a pith chambered between the nodes. Buds brown, about ⅛ inch long, rounded or slightly pointed, with about 4 scales.

Bark — Thin and tight, green at first, becoming darker at maturity and often covered with wartlike bumps.

Sweet Leaf is an uncommon understory tree found throughout the East Texas Piney Woods. It prefers moist sites, being associated with creeks, streams, and adjacent woods. Browsing animals, especially horses, are fond of the sweet thickish leaves, and birds quickly eat the fleshy fruits. Humans also benefit from the plant. The leaves were formerly used to dye wool yellow, and a medicinal tincture was made from the root bark. Sweet Leafs are uncommon in cultivation, mainly because they are difficult to propagate or transplant from the wild. They are a handsome, virtually evergreen, tree with attractive flowers and foliage. They are most prominent during the late fall when the leaves stand out or in very early spring when the flowers steal the show. In the Sabine National Forest grows the state champion Sweet Leaf with a trunk girth of 22 inches, total height of 45 feet, and covering an area 24 feet across.

226

ANACAHUITA

Cordia boissieri.
Mexican Olive, Wild Olive.
A small tree or shrub with a rounded crown rarely over 25 feet with showy white flowers and velvety leaves.

Leaves — Soft velvety, 4-5 inches long, 3-4 inches wide, light to dark green often with light brown fuzz on the underside.
Flowers — Showy white with a spot of yellow in the throat, 1 inch long, 2 inches wide.
Fruit — A drupe, round, 1 inch long, shiny, white to pale yellow turning yellowish brown, calyx enclosing fruit is ribbed. The single, long seed is somewhat spindle-shaped and about ¾ of an inch in length.
Twigs — Brown to grayish, fuzzy.
Bark — Gray, often tinged with red, broken into irregular flat ridges.

227

The Anacahuita is an attractive tree growing wild deep in the brushlands and thickets of South Texas and northern Mexico. Because of its showy flowers, it is often planted as an ornamental in the Lower Rio Grande Valley and Mexico. Anacahuita is occasionally planted as far north as San Antonio where it freezes back to the ground in cold winters. A nice specimen covered with blossoms during the warmer months can be seen in front of the Alamo in San Antonio where it grows 10 to 15 feet high. The plant has a number of common names, including Mexican Olive, Texas Olive, Flor de Anacahuite, Nacahuite, and Nacahuitl, the latter two derived from the Nahuatl Indian name *Anacuahuitl* meaning paper tree. The genus name, *Cordia,* is from the German pharmacist and botanist Valerius Cordus, and the species name, *boissieri,* from the botanist Boissier.

The fruit is sweet and pulpy, and although edible it is said to cause dizziness if eaten in excess. In Mexico, a jelly from the fruit is used as a remedy for coughs. The leaves are an old home cure for rheumatism and bronchial disorders. In the 1860's, the wood even attracted attention in Germany as a possible remedy for tuberculosis. The fruit is also quite palatable to birds and other wildlife. Birds often use these trees for nesting sites. Although not used commercially, the wood is occasionally made into small woodenware objects. Another Cordia species called Geiger Tree *(C. sebestena)* is similar but has orange flowers and grows in Southern Florida and the Caribbean basin.

228

ANAQUA

Ehretia anacua.
Knock-Away, Sandpaper Tree.
A medium sized tree or shrub with a dense crown. The white flower clusters in early spring are followed by small orange fruit.

Leaves — Olive to dark green, 2-4 inches long, oval to oblong, pointed at the tip, margins often toothed from the middle to the tip. Very rough on the upper surface, usually somewhat evergreen.
Flowers — Small, white, clustered at the ends of branches, fragrant, blooms early spring.
Fruit — Spherical, ¼ to ⅓ inches in diameter, orange or yellow, produced in clusters, fleshy, edible.
Twigs — Brown to gray, often fuzzy when young.
Bark — Gray to reddish brown, becoming furrowed with age.

229

The Anaqua is an attractive tree primarily native to South Texas and Mexico but found growing along streams as far north as Austin. Although the Anaqua takes on a shrubby appearance on dry hillsides, it can also reach heights of 50 feet along streams and river valleys. Anaqua is one of the dominant species of the evergreen woodland of the Lower Rio Grande Valley at the southern tip of Texas. This tree, along with Ebony, Tepeguaje, and in a few areas the Sabal Palm, give this region a subtropical air. It is an attractive tree, often planted for shade in South Texas. Although it is sometimes cultivated as far north as Dallas, it will freeze back in cold winters there. The rough texture of the leaf, due to minute stiff hairs, has given rise to the name Sand-

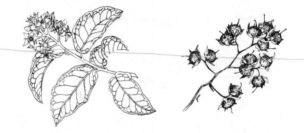

paper Tree. The scientific name, *Ehretia,* is for George Dionysius Ehret, a German botanical artist. The species name, *anaqua,* also a common name, is an Indian word. In the German-settled New Braunfels area, the tree is called *Vogelbeerenbaum,* meaning "Birdberry Tree", because birds love the sweet yellow or orangish fruit. The wood of Anaqua is heavy and close grained. It has been used to make wheel spokes and axles, fence posts and tool handles.

The national champion Anaqua can be found in the courtyard of the Plaza San Antonio hotel in downtown San Antonio. This tree's vital statistics are a cumulative trunk circumference of 175 inches, height of 42 feet, and it shades an area 46 feet across. The former champion, often called the "Mission Anaqua," grows in Refugio on the site of the original Refugio Mission.

EASTERN REDBUD

Cercis canadensis.
Judas Tree.
Small tree to about 40 feet tall with a spreading, flat or slightly rounded crown.

Leaves — Alternate, simple, deciduous, 3-5 inches long, turning yellow in autumn. Dark green on top, lighter below and slightly hairy. The distinctive heart-shaped leaves are considered by some to represent a terminal leaflet reduced to a vestige from a compound leaf lineage.
Flowers — In early spring, before or with the unfurling leaves. The pink pea-like flowers are about ½ inch in length and appear in clusters of 4-8 on older branches and often along the trunk.

231

Fruit — Clusters of flattened papery pods 2-4 inches in length ripening in the fall. The dark brown shiny seeds are about ¼ inch long.

Twigs — Slender, slightly zigzag; brown, smooth, and shiny at first, becoming gray later. Leaf buds tiny, dark brown scaly, flower buds on older twigs and branches larger than the leaf buds, somewhat cylindrical and appressed to the twig.

Bark — Thin and tight, reddish brown when young, turning gray and smooth but eventually becoming scaly and separating into narrow ridges.

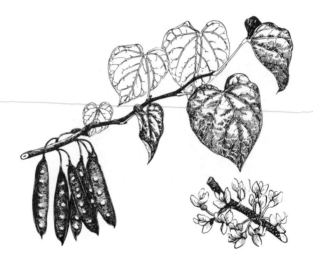

Conspicuous early spring flowers make this one of the most attractive and popular native plants used as an ornamental. Native redbuds are fast growing, having few pest or disease problems, and are found naturally throughout most of the state except South Texas.

Eastern Redbud is typically found in the understory of upland woods, along stream banks, and at the edge of woods throughout East Texas. Its wood is attractive and durable but generally too small to be of much value other than for specialty items. The flower buds, flowers, and tender fruit pods are all edible; they are probably at their best sauteed in butter for about 10 minutes. The flower buds are also reported to be tasty when pickled, and the raw flowers can be eaten in salads. Redbuds are also known in general as "Judas Trees" but this particularly refers to the Mediterranean species *Cercis siliquestrum*. The name comes from the story that Judas supposedly hung himself from one of these trees.

TEXAS REDBUD. *Cercis canadensis* var. *texensis.*

This Redbud differs from the other natives in that the leaves are relatively thicker, dull bluish and leathery or shiny dark green on top with smooth twigs and leaf stalks. It is found throughout Central and North Central Texas on limestone soils.

MEXICAN REDBUD. *Cercis canadensis* var. *mexicana.*

The leaves of this tree resemble Texas Redbud but differ in having densely hairy twigs and leaf stalks. In Texas it is primarily found in the Trans-Pecos mountains.

HONEY LOCUST.

Gleditsia triacanthos.
Medium to large sized tree to about 70 feet tall and 30 inches in trunk diameter. The short trunk usually divides into two to several large ascending branches that form a graceful spreading crown with drooping branch tips.

Leaves — Alternate, deciduous, single or twice compound with 15 to 30 oval or oblong leaves about 1½ inch long and half as wide, occasionally slightly toothed, dull bluish green turning yellow in autumn.
Flowers — In spring, after the leaves are nearly grown, small greenish-yellow flowers in the axils of the leaves.

234

Fruit — Maturing in the fall and persisting most of the winter. Red-brown pods about one foot long, one inch wide curling spirally as it dries, causing it to roll in the wind after dropping and spreading numerous ⅓-inch-long dark brown seeds.

Twigs — Slender to stoutish, slightly zigzagged, green to reddish brown, often armed with red-brown straight or three-branched thorns up to 3 inches in length.

Bark — Smooth at first, gray to gray brown becoming somewhat fissured and broken in longitudinal plates with projecting edges. The trunk is often armed with terrifying chestnut-brown single or three-branched thorns up to one foot in length.

Honey Locust is a fast-growing, sun-loving tree seldom found in the understory but usually as a pioneer on cuts or fence lines. It is at home in creek bottoms or on dry hills where it becomes more shrubby. Honey Locust is found naturally in the eastern third of Texas southwest to Bexar County. Isolated native populations exist in Armstrong, Tom Green, and Brazoria counties, but Honey Locust is widely known across the state as an ornamental or shade tree. Most popular are the thornless varieties (*G. triacanthos* var. *inermis*) which have been developed into several selections. Honey Locust make good street and ornamental trees because of their fast growth, light shade, disease and drought-resistance, and the deep root system that does not lift up pavement. The thin bark, however, makes the tree very susceptible to injury from fire or mowing equipment.

235

Cattle eagerly eat the sweet pods. They can contain as much as thirty percent sugar—higher than sugar beets. Indians ate the honey-like substance in young pods between the seeds and sucked the sweetness from the coating on the seeds. The awesome thorns were used for fishing-spear tips by the Indians, and by pioneers for carding wool and pinning sacks—or even clothes, in a pinch. Cherokee Indians made bows from the strong wood but settlers valued it primarily for fence posts and railroad ties before the days of preservative wood treatments. Honey Locust wood is durable and strong under pressure. The sapwood is yellowish and the heartwood is light red to red brown but the grain is too coarse for most uses. Bees feed on the small flowers and a few species of wildlife enjoy the seed pods.

WATER LOCUST. *Gleditsia aquatica.*

Occurs mainly in East Texas along river bottoms that are periodically flooded, with other slough species such as Bald Cypress and Water Tupelo. It differs from Honey Locust by having a smaller 1- to 3-seeded pod about 1-2 inches long and generally smaller leaves. The wood takes a better polish than that of Honey Locust but the tree is usually scrawny and little used commercially.

TEXAS HONEY LOCUST. *Gleditsia texana.*

Usually found in the Brazos River bottoms and considered to be a naturally occurring hybrid between Honey and Water Locusts. The national champion Texas Honey Locust is located on the Alabama-Coushatta Indian Reservation near Livingston in Polk County. It is 112 feet tall, and has a trunk circumference of 81 inches and a crown spread of 43 feet.

RETAMA

Parkinsonia aculeata.
Jerusalem Thorn, Paloverde.
A thorny, green-barked shrub or tree to 35 feet with a drooping rounded crown and fragrant yellow flowers.

Leaves — Twice compound, numerous tiny leaflets on a long flat rachis 8 to 16 inches long. Leaflets often drop, leaving a bare rachis.
Flowers— Showy yellow, 5-petaled, one with a tinge of orange, borne in loose drooping clusters 5-6 inches long. Blooms sporadically throughout the spring and summer.
Fruit — A narrow pod 2-4 inches long, light brown to reddish, constricted between the seeds.
Twigs — Green to yellowish, stout and thorny.
Bark — Thin, smooth, green turning brown later with thin scales.

The Retama is an attractive tree with drooping foliage native to South and West Texas. It is reported as far north

237

as Williamson County, west to Arizona, and down into South America. Retama is often found in poorly drained areas but can occur on a variety of sites. Because this tree has green bark and branches, it is often called *Paloverde* (Spanish for "green stick") although this name usually refers to *Cercidium* spp. Another of its many common names is *Lluvia de Oro,* meaning "shower of gold," referring to the vivid yellow blossoms adorning this tree in spring and summer. "Jerusalem thorn" and "Barbados flower fence" are names sometimes used in the tropics where Retama is used as a hedge.

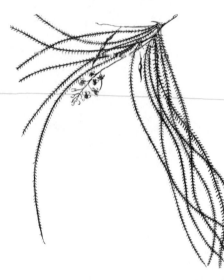

Retama wood is light brown with a yellow sapwood. It is hard and close grained. Occasionally it is used for fuel and has at times been utilized for paper making. Livestock browse the foliage and branches during rough times. Bees are attracted to the flowers, and the pods are sought after as food by deer and other animals. In earlier times the pods were pounded and made into a coarse flour by Indians. In Mexico a tea brewed from the branches and leaves is used in the treatment of diabetes and as a fever remedy. Retama is an attractive plant cultivated as an ornamental but can become a pest in disturbed areas.

BLACK LOCUST

Robinia pseudoacacia.

Medium sized tree to about 50 feet tall with a trunk about 12 inches in diameter. The trunk is frequently twisted or crooked and divides into several branches supporting an irregular open crown.

Leaves — Alternate, deciduous, single compound about 8-14 inches in overall length. Leaflets 7-19, individuals 1½ to 2 inches in length and ½ to ¾ inch wide, dark green and somewhat bluish tinged on top, paler beneath, turning yellow in fall. Leaves fold up at night or during rains.
Flowers — In spring after the leaves have unfolded, white, fragrant pea-like flowers about 1 inch long appear in hanging clusters up to 5 inches in length.
Fruit — Maturing in the fall but persisting through much of the winter, flat, light-brown pods 3-4 inches in length enclosing 4-8 kidney-shaped seeds per pod.

239

Twigs — Greenish brown, somewhat stout, and slightly zigzagged with a pair of short spines up to ½ inch in length
at the base of each leaf.
Bark — Thick, coarse, greenish at first, becoming dark reddish
to nearly black with distinctive long, interlacing rounded
ridges and deep furrows.

Black Locust is not originally native to Texas but has been
widely planted and naturalized here. Its fast growth the first
20 to 30 years, attractive flowers, and ability to build up the
soil with the nitrogen-fixing roots make it desirable as an
ornamental and for erosion control. However, the locust
borer, which devastates young trees, and the weedy characteristic of suckering from the roots are drawbacks. In one
area of East Texas it was found that native pines stabilized
the soil better than Black Locust. Only the wood remains
highly valued. It is heavy, hard, close grained, turns well,
and takes a high polish. There is very little light-colored sapwood; it is almost all greenish-yellow heartwood.

Used as a structural beam, Black Locust is one of the
strongest hardwoods in North America and is also one of
the most durable native woods. These qualities, plus its low
shrinkage when drying, made it ideal for ship nails. It was
the preferred wood for fence posts, railroad ties, mine timbers, rake teeth, wagon hubs, and is still the only wood used
as insulator pins for electric lines. As a firewood only Hickory can come close to its output. A cultivar, Shipmost
Locust, grows much straighter and with very little trunk
branching except near the top. The flowers can be eaten as
fritters, but the roots, bark, leaves, and seeds are considered
poisonous. Black Locust still has some value for stabilizing and rebuilding spoil banks where it can sucker freely,
providing shelter for wildlife.

240

TEXAS MOUNTAIN LAUREL

Sophora secundiflora.
Mescal Bean, Frijollito.
A small to medium sized evergreen tree up to 30 feet with violet, sweet-scented flowers.

Leaves — Dark green, lustrous, waxlike, leaflets oblong 1-2 inches long.

Flowers — Showy violet in clusters at the tip of branches, occasionally white, fragrant; individual flowers pea-like.

241

Fruit — A pod 3½ to 5 inches long, hard, constricted, containing hard shiny red seeds ¾ to 1 inch in diameter when mature.

Twigs — Velvety green when young, later with dark splotches and becoming brown with age.

Bark — Dark gray to black, with narrow ridges and shallow fissures.

The Texas Mountain Laurel is found growing on limestone soils of Central Texas, West Texas, and into southern New Mexico. It also grows on gravelly hills in parts of South Texas and down through northern Mexico. Although often called Mountain Laurel, this tree is not related to the Mountain Laurel of the eastern U.S., *Kalmia latifolia*, or the true Laurel, *Laurus nobilis*.

The Mountain Laurel, or Mescal Bean as many call it, is an attractive tree cultivated for its evergreen foliage and showy spring flowers. These violet flowers have a sweet fragrance resembling grape Kool Aid. It is said that a bouquet of them left in the bedroom overnight will make one nauseated. Bees are found busy at work on the blossoms each spring, but the honey is considered by some to be mildly poisonous.

242

The fruit pods contain shiny red or orange seeds when ripe. Archeological remains indicate a ceremonial use of the seeds dating before A.D. 1000. They were often ground and small amounts mixed with mescal, an alcoholic beverage made from the Century Plant (*Agave* sp.) to make it more intoxicating, and this association has given the seeds the name. Mescal Beans have been used to induce visions, as a divinatory agent to predict the future, and as a stimulant and ritual emetic in other ceremonies. In 1539 Cabeza de Vaca reported the use of mescal beans as trade items among the Texas Indians. A strand of beans 6 feet long was said to buy a small horse in areas to the north. On the Stephen Long expedition in 1820, it was reported that the Arapaho and Iowa Indians used the beans as a narcotic and a medicine; they were thought magical, with the ability to multiply, and were often worn as amulets to protect the wearer from bodily harm.

The mescal beans are quite poisonous; they contain the alkaloid cystine, which is a toxic pyrridine causing nausea, convulsions, and sometimes death. One bean is said to be fatal to human beings. If swallowed whole, however, they usually pass through the system causing no harm. To avert the danger, the peyote cactus gradually replaced the mescal bean for use in ceremonial practices, but the red bean was still used in the ceremonial dress of the leader in the form of buttons and necklaces.

The Texas Mountain Laurel is widely planted as an ornamental. If you are interested in growing the Texas Mountain Laurel and are not in any hurry to have a specimen tree, the seeds can best be germinated by planting them when they are a little immature (slightly pink) or by nicking the hard seed coat with a file. The national champion is growing in Comal County. It is 27 feet tall and has an average crown spread of 27 feet and a trunk girth of 68 inches.

EVE'S NECKLACE

Sophora affinis.
Texas Sophora, Necklace Tree.
A deciduous tree usually to 20 feet
with a round top crown.

Leaves — Bright green, 6-9 inches long, made up of 13-18 oval
 leaflets, 1 inch long.
Flowers — Pinkish white, in drooping clusters, 3-5 inches long.
Fruit — A black pod ½ to 4 inches long, tightly constricted be-
 tween the seeds, 4-8 black seeds.
Twigs — Green to brown; young branches light green, turn-
 ing brownish later.
Bark — Brown to gray, scaly with age.

Eve's Necklace is found growing in limestone soils of Central and Northeast Texas on fence rows, hillsides, and along streams or ravines. A relative of the Texas Mountain Laurel, it is fairly common around Central Texas but many are unaware of it. Unlike the Mountain Laurel, this tree is deciduous. The Eve's Necklace blossom hangs in a cluster of delicate rosy-pink flowers. During the late summer and fall the plant is loaded with black bean pods which are constricted at each seed giving the appearance of a string of

beads, hence the common names Eve's Necklace and Necklace Tree. The seeds, however, are black and contain poisonous alkaloids. Ring-tailed cats are known to eat the fruits, and the foliage is often browsed by deer and livestock. The wood is light red or dark brownish with a bright yellow sapwood. It is dense, hard, and yields a yellow dye.

Eve's Necklace has ornamental potential and can be seen in some yard plantings around the state. Some trees are known to sucker from the roots forming small thickets. The national champion Eve's Necklace grows in San Antonio. It stands 50 feet tall with an 80 inch circumference and has a crown spread of 50 feet.

Fabaceae - Legume Family

CATCLAW ACACIA

Acacia wrightii.
Uña de Gato.
Shrub or small tree to 25 feet tall with a rounded flattened crown and an often leaning trunk about 1 foot in diameter.

Leaves — Alternate or sometimes clustered, twice compound, 1-2 inches long with 1-3 pairs of pinna each with 2-6 pairs of leaflets ¼ to ½ inch long, smooth or slightly hairy.

Flowers — Early to mid spring or later after heavy rains, in cylindrical spikes about 1 inch or more in length and ½ inch thick consisting of many small flowers that are mostly numerous stamens roughly ¼ inch long.

Fruit — Maturing in midsummer to early fall, as a flattened pod 1-6 inches long that is often slightly curved and somewhat pinched between the seeds which are thin, light brown, and about ¼ inch in length.

Twigs — Gray or brown and slender, often armed with short recurved spines about ¼ inch long.

246

Bark — Thin and gray brown when young, becoming thicker and soon dividing into flat ridges and shallow fissures which become deeper with maturity.

Catclaw Acacia is a typical member of the South Texas scrub forests along with Prickly Pear and Mesquite. There are quite a number of these that can be seen rising out of brush around the Uvalde area. The wood is heavy, hard, and very attractive with a white sapwood and red or reddish-brown heartwood but is generally used for fence posts or firewood. Indians used the ground-up seeds to make a flour, and a substance similar to the commercial gum arabic is often exuded from the trunk and branches. Honeybees make an excellent honey from the flowers, and many species of wildlife eat the seeds. This could be a good ornamental tree for arid areas that are normally deprived of natural shade. The national champion Catclaw Acacia is located in Uvalde County. It is 36 feet tall, has a trunk girth of 72 inches, and covers an area 42 feet across.

CATCLAW. *Acacia greggii.*

A shrub or small tree to about 30 feet tall that is very difficult to distinguish from *Acacia wrightii* but differing by having twisted seed pods, leaflets usually less than ¼ inch in length, and a broader range extending into the Trans-Pecos area and the Panhandle as far north as Taylor County.

247

CATCLAW. *Acacia roemeriana.*
Roemer's Acacia.

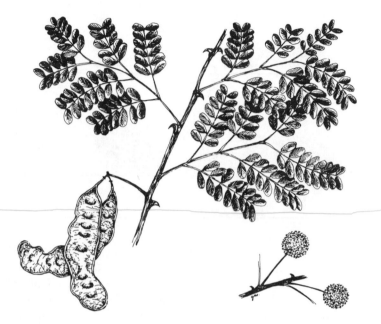

A shrub or small tree separated from the above species by having flowers in round instead of cylindrical clusters. It can be found from Travis County northwest to Jones County, southwest to Maverick County and west to the southern Trans-Pecos area. The national champion Roemer's Catclaw is 17 feet tall, has a trunk circumference of 26 inches, and a crown spread of 18 feet. It is growing in Comal County.

HUISACHE

Acacia farnesiana.
[*Acacia smallii*]. Sweet Acacia.
A small tree or large shrub to about
30 feet tall with a spreading rounded
or flattened crown.

Leaves — Feather-like, 1-4 inches long, leaflets about 1 / 10 inch
   in length, bright green or gray green appearing hairy under magnification.
Flowers — Borne in early spring in rounded, densely-flowered
   heads. Bright yellow and very fragrant.
Fruit — Midsummer to early fall, woody pods 1-2 inches long,
   brown to almost black. Each pod contains two rows of
   several shiny, hard, gray seeds that are often eaten by
   weevils before they mature.
Twigs — Armed with paired, straight, white spines 1-3 inches
   long at the base of each leaf.
Bark — Reddish brown, thin when young, forming narrow
   ridges and furrows when older.

Fabaceae - Legume Family

Huisache (pronounced "*Wee*-satch" or "Wee-satch-eh") is a fast growing pioneer type found throughout South and South Central Texas and extending eastward to the areas of Crockett and Houston. It prefers low moist sites but can be found virtually anywhere throughout its range where it can get ample sunshine. There seem to be two growth forms of Huisache: coastal plants tend to have a single trunk with somewhat drooping branches; inland plants usually have several trunks with ascending branches. The flowers appear in very early spring, and in South Central Texas are often caught by late frosts that freeze their buds off. Huisache wood looks a lot like mesquite and is sometimes

confused with it. This can spoil a barbecue because Huisache imparts a slightly unpleasant taste to the food. Cattle that eat too many young tender branches are likely to produce bad-tasting meat. The spiny twigs can be a real hazard to foot traffic and pneumatic tires. As a landscape plant, Huisache has a cult following for its feathery foliage, fragrant showy flowers, fast growth, and spreading flat-topped form. On the other hand, the trunk often branches low to the ground with narrow crotch angles that usually split later, the flowers often freeze, and the spines are an annoyance.

250

Huisache plays an important role in nature by providing quick shade and protection on disturbed sites, thereby serving as a "nurse tree" for many species of shrubs and cacti. This is a tree of many uses. The pods were formerly made into ink, the juice was used as a glue for mending pottery, and the bark for dying skins. Various parts of the tree have local medicinal value. Decoctions from the green fruit serve as an astringent and the roots were used as a treatment for tuberculosis. Wound dressings were made from the crushed leaves, and the flowers were used as an infusion for indigestion and as an ointment for curing headaches. The national champion Huisache is 36 feet tall and has a trunk circumference of 97 inches and a crown spread of 51 feet. It is growing in Zapata County.

This plant also occurs in southern Florida, the West Indies, Central America, and northern South America. It is plantation grown in southern France for the aromatic flowers which are used as a perfume base.

PALOVERDE

Cercidium macrum.
Border Paloverde.
A shrub or small tree with a green trunk and branches growing to 20 feet.

Leaves — Twice compound with 2-4 pairs of oblong leaflets 3 inches long.
Flowers — Yellow, pea-like, 5 petals, the largest spotted with red.
Fruit — A pod 1 to 2½ inches long, ½ inch wide, flattened, containing 1-5 shiny compressed seeds.
Twigs — Light green turning dark green or brown later, armed with straight or slightly curved spines.
Bark — Thin, smooth, greenish.

This small tree with spiny crooked branches and attractive yellow flowers is native to South Texas and northeastern Mexico in clay and sandy soils. Because of its southern range, it is often called Border Paloverde. This is a plant well adapted to arid or semi-arid environments. During drought conditions it sheds its leaves, thus avoiding excess water loss due to evapo-transpiration. The trunk and branches,

252

which are green (containing chlorophyll), can still carry out photosynthesis although the leaves are shed. The root system of the Paloverde is also well suited to drought conditions. It not only puts down a deep taproot to soak up ground water but also sends out shallow surface roots to take advantage of rainfall and surface runoff.

The attractive yellow flowers of the Paloverde are sought by bees. Cattle will eat the fruit pods which also make a palatable meal or flour when ground. Jackrabbits and other small mammals occasionally browse the foliage. The genus name *Cercidium* is derived from *kerkidion*, Greek for "weaver's comb" to which the pods have a slight resemblance. Paloverde wood is sometimes used for fuel.

TEXAS PALOVERDE. *Cercidium texanum.*

This species differs by having a more shrublike form and fewer leaflets (1-2). It occurs in the vicinity of Langtry and Del Rio, and seems to intergrade with Border Paloverde where their ranges overlap.

253

GOLDEN BALL LEAD TREE

Leucaena retusa.
Wahoo Tree.
A shrub or small tree usually to 15 feet
without spines or thorns.

Leaves — 3 to 8 inches long with 3-5 pairs of pinnae and 3-8 pairs
   of leaflets which are usually oblong, ⅓ to 1 inch long,
   notched at the tip or with a small extended round tip.
   Glands often present.
Flowers — Bright yellow, densely clustered in rounded heads,
   ½ to 1½ inches in diameter, fragrant. Blooms sporadically,
   late spring through fall.
Fruit — Long and narrow, flattened, 4-10 inches long, brown;
   seed round and flat, lustrous brown.
Twigs — Brown or reddish.
Bark — Light gray to brownish, smooth when young, developing cracks or fissures later.

254

The Golden Ball Lead Tree is a small, lean tree of the legume family found on dry, rocky limestone soils on the western part of the Edwards Plateau and the Trans-Pecos. It also ranges into southern New Mexico and south into Coahuila, Mexico. A number of these trees can be seen on the hillsides in and around Garner State Park near Concan. They are also quite prevalent between Sanderson and Fort Stockton, in areas of Big Bend, and in the Davis Mountains. The Lead Tree is most noticeable in late spring to early summer and sporadically through the fall when the bright yellow or golden blossoms are present. It is very palatable to

cattle and deer and is often browsed down on hillsides. The wood is very brittle. The Golden Ball Lead Tree is quite attractive and suitable for cultivation on dry sites. These plants are easily grown from seed which can be planted as soon as acquired or stored for several years. The national champion Golden Ball Lead Tree is growing in Terrell County. It is 21 feet tall, with a crown spread of 26 feet and a trunk circumference of 33 inches.

TEPEGUAJE

Leucaena pulverulenta.
Mexican Lead Tree.
A mimosa-like tree with a tall, straight trunk and a rounded, spreading crown up to 50 feet tall.

Leaves — Bright green, alternate, compound, fernlike, 10 inches long with 10 pairs of pinnae and 15-50 pairs of leaflets.

Flowers — White, densely clustered in rounded heads, ½ to ¾ inch across.

Fruit — Narrow, flattened, 5 to 12 inches long, containing shiny brown seeds.

Twigs — Fuzzy, white, becoming pale brown.

Bark — Gray to light reddish brown.

256

Tepeguaje is a fast growing tree found on rich, moist soils along streams, resacas, and river banks in extreme South Texas and adjacent Mexico. It often grows alongside the Texas Ebony, Tenaza, Anaqua, and some brushland species near the Rio Grande River. This unique subtropical community, however, is quickly being replaced by cultivated fields. The Tepeguaje is a large and attractive tree, often planted for shade in Brownsville and nearby towns. It is occasionally planted as far north as San Antonio, but it is cold-sensitive and will freeze there in severe winters. During the winter of 1983, many of them froze to the ground in the

Lower Rio Grande Valley but have quickly regrown. The white flowers of the Tepeguaje are fragrant and very attractive to honeybees. In Mexico, the flat, shiny seeds are occasionally used for making necklaces. Tepeguaje wood is heavy and close grained and for this reason often called Lead Tree. The rich, dark-brown wood is considered valuable in Mexico and used for lumber. The national champion stands 43 feet tall and is growing at Hoopy's R.V. Park in Alamo, Texas.

TEXAS EBONY

Pithecellobium ebano.
[*Pithecellobium flexicaule*].
A dark green spiny shrub or tree with irregular spreading branches found growing at the southern tip of Texas and in Mexico.

Leaves — Thick, lustrous, dark green, 2-3 pairs of pinnae and 3-6 pairs of leaflets; leaflets oblong or obovate.

Flowers — Cream or yellow in spikes 1-2 inches long. Blooms June to August.

Fruit — Thick, woody, curved pod, 4-6 inches long with brown seeds.

Twigs — Reddish brown to gray with short paired spines.

Bark — Dark brown to black.

258

This densely foliaged tree armed with spines is widely known in the Lower Rio Grande Valley. Although often a shrub, it will reach heights of up to 40 feet in wooded areas along the Rio Grande River. The Ebony, which usually retains its leaves during the winter in extreme South Texas, is a common yard tree in the Brownsville and McAllen area. The cream or yellow flowers appearing in the spring are attractive and very fragrant. Following them are thick, woody curved pods that have given rise to the name Ape's Earrings.

In Mexico, the green seeds are cooked and eaten; when ripe, they can be roasted and eaten or ground into a substitute for coffee. They can also be popped like popcorn. These seeds are very high in crude protein and are eaten by deer, javelinas, and small mammals. White-tailed deer also favor the high-protein foliage for browse.

The Ebony wood is dark red to purplish brown with yellow sapwood. It is durable and used for fence posts, fuel, cabinets, wagons, and small woodenware objects. The seeds are sometimes made into jewelry. The border town of Los Ebanos is named for these trees lining the Rio Grande. Los Ebanos is the site of a hand-pulled ferryboat for crossing the river—in fact the only government-operated ferry of its kind in the U.S. A big, beautiful old Ebony tree supports the ferry with a cable on the U.S. side.

The national champion Ebony Tree is found in McAllen and stands 40 feet tall with a 133-inch circumference and a crown spread of 44 feet.

TENAZA. *Pithecellobium pallens.*

A shrub or occasionally a small tree up to 30 feet tall. Although closely related to Texas Ebony, it is quite different in appearance, having light green fernlike foliage with a pair of short spines at the base of each leaf. Flowers are yellowish to white in round or semi-round heads. The seed

pods are 2 to 5 inches long, straight, flattened except where the seeds bulge, and pointed at the tip. Seeds are flattened and lustrous brown to black. This plant grows in Mexico and in extreme South Texas and northward along the coast to San Patricio County. It is considered a weedy pest by most local residents.

MESQUITE

Prosopis glandulosa.
Honey Mesquite.
Shrub, or tree to 40 feet tall with a broad open crown and a short trunk about 18 inches in diameter.

Leaves — Alternate, deciduous, up to 10 inches in length and doubly compound with one pair of pinnae each, with 7-20 leaflets up to 2 inches long and about ¼ inch in width.

Flowers — Mainly in late spring but continuing sporadically throughout summer. Consisting of many small yellowish flowers in elongated spikes arranged in small clusters arising from the leaf axils.

Fruit — Maturing in late summer or early fall as slightly flattened tan pods up to 10 inches long and about ⅜ inch wide; the brown seeds are imbedded in a soft spongy substance and completely covered by a thin papery envelope.

261

Twigs— Thin to moderately stout and slightly zigzagged, dark green to dark brown, sometimes thornless but usually armed with a single or a pair of stiff, straight, sharp, whitish spines up to 2 inches long.

Bark— Thin and reddish brown at first but eventually becoming grayish with deep fissures and thick ridges.

Mesquite is quite common throughout most of Texas except the Piney Woods where it occurs as isolated populations. It can be found on many different sites throughout its range but generally reaches its best development along creeks or river bottoms. Authorities do not agree on the prehistoric range of Mesquite. Some say the tree migrated here from Mexico following the cattle herds as they ate the pods and spread the undigested seeds. Others maintain the tree has been here all along and is now proliferating as a result of land mismanagement. Whatever the case, Mesquite now "infests" millions of acres, often creating dense thickets that restrict land use. Early travelers often wrote about the "peach orchard" effect produced by the Mesquite savannah they traveled through in South Central Texas.

262

Mesquite are extremely tenacious, sprouting readily from the root crown and sending roots 100 feet or more down in pursuit of water. Actually, these trees are not all bad. They perform a service by fixing nitrogen in the soil, as has been proven by scientific testing. (You can note for yourself that shrubs under a Mesquite are often bigger and healthier than those elsewhere in the area.)

Mesquite wood is somewhat heavy, hard, and strong with a thick reddish-brown heartwood and a thin yellowish sapwood. It has long been underrated in Texas where it was formerly used almost entirely for fence posts, railroad ties, and wagon wheels, hubs, and spokes. Recently it has come into its own for such things as attractive flooring, gunstocks, and furniture. There is even an organization, "Los Amigos del Mesquite," which recognizes the wood and many other useful aspects of Mesquite.

Throughout much of its range this is the only tree large enough to be a source of shade and fuel or timber—especially for use as building beams. Mesquite wood makes excellent fuel as it burns evenly with a hot flame and leaves behind good coals. For cooking, Mesquite imparts a distinctive and delicious flavor rivaled only by Hickory. It is an excellent wood for barbecue and has achieved international acclaim, becoming quite the rage in many fancy restaurants. The fruit pulp contains a relatively high sugar content and was part of the Indian diet. Meal from the seeds was made into cakes and also fermented into an alcoholic beverage. The flowers provide a good bee food and were sometimes eaten by the Indians. A gum exudate from the bark was eaten like candy or dissolved in water and used for treating dysentery, sore throat, and open wounds. Later, Texans would export this gum by the thousands of pounds annually back east for the production of gum drops and mucilage. Rough cordage was made from the root bark after soaking it thoroughly in water. Because Mesquite leafs out late, the sign of those leaves popping out is usually a good indicator that spring has arrived and all danger of frost is past. Many species of wildlife depend on Mesquite for food and shelter from the sun. The national champion Mesquite has a trunk circumference of 152 inches, is 52 feet tall, and has a crown spread of 71 feet. It is growing in Real County.

SCREWBEAN MESQUITE. *Prosopis pubescens.* Tornillo.

This plant differs from Honey Mesquite by having only 5 to 8 pairs of leaflets, the bean is tightly spirally coiled, and the twigs are gray instead of brownish red. It is usually found along river valleys in West Texas where it often forms

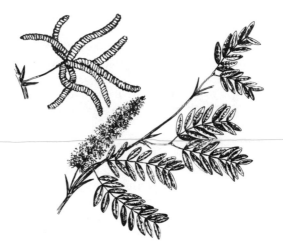

dense thickets. Screwbean shares many of the same qualities as Honey Mesquite in regard to uses of the wood, fruits, and medicinal properties. The national champion Screwbean Mesquite is 30 feet tall and has a crown spread of 36 feet and a trunk circumference of 39 inches. It is growing in Big Bend National Park, Brewster County.

SILK TREE

Albizia julibrissin.
Mimosa Tree.
Small tree to about 30 feet tall with a wide-spreading crown and a short trunk 1 foot in diameter.

Leaves — Alternate, deciduous, compound, 10-15 inches long, with leaflets ¼ to ⅜ inch in length. Graceful feather-like leaves that tend to fold up at night, in the rain, or under drought stress.

Flowers — Borne mid to late spring and summer in fluffy clusters of pink heads that get their color from the masses of stamens.

Fruit — Thin papery pods 3-½ to 8 inches long with several hard, flattened, brown shiny seeds.

Twigs — Green at first, becoming gray to brown later with a prominent stipular scar.

Bark — Tight and thin, smooth and gray.

Silk Tree is a native of China and temperate Asia where the wood is used in cabinetmaking, the aromatic foliage in medicine, as green manure, and the flowers occasionally employed as powder puffs by local women. The tree has become naturalized in the eastern part of Texas and can be

265

found growing along roadside ditches. Even though it has escaped cultivation, it has not become as pestiferous as some other naturalized exotics such as Chinaberry or Tallow Tree.

Silk Tree is a fast growing familiar ornamental with a lovely growth habit, delicate fern-like foliage, and showy pink powder-puff-like flowers which cover its crown in the spring. It was widely planted throughout the South in the

1950's but has been declining in use and is seldom planted today—mainly because of a fungal disease known as Mimosa wilt, which has devasted this species from New York south to Florida and west to Texas. Trees infected will often wilt and die within a year's time, and no successful cure or prevention has been found; however, resistant varieties have recently been developed.

During their heyday of popularity, specimen Silk Trees would often be severely pruned during the dormant season. This would result in vigorous, long, arching branchlets giving the plant a palmlike or prehistoric look.

GUAYACAN

Guaiacum angustifolium.
[*Porlieria angustifolia*].
Soapbush.
An evergreen plant with short irregular branches. Usually a shrub but occasionally a small tree to 20 feet.

Leaves — Thick, leathery, dark green, 4-8 pairs of small leaflets, evergreen.
Flowers — Purple, ⅓ to ¾ inch across in small clusters mildly fragrant, consisting of 5 petals and sepals with 10 stamens.
Fruit — A heart-shaped capsule with protruding winged margins, encloses 1-3 shiny red or orange seeds.
Twigs — Gray, stiff.
Bark — Gray to black, smooth and relatively thin.

This compact plant with thick leathery leaves is native to South and West Texas and occasionally seen north to Austin. It is a common component of the South Texas brush

267

country and south into northern Mexico. The dark green leaves of the Guayacan which are retained during the winter really stand out amongst the other shrub species. The fragrant flowers appearing the first of spring are showy purple or violet. The Guayacan is a good source of early honey in the Rio Grande Valley, and is also found growing in northern Mexico. One common name, Soap Bush, is derived from the use of its root bark sold in Mexican markets as a kind of *amole* or soap which is valued for washing wool because it does not fade colors. Extracts of the root have also been used to cure various ailments.

Guayacan wood is very heavy and considered one of the hardest native Texas woods. It is related to the Lignumvitae of commerce which is used to build ship bearings, among other things, because of its qualities of being hard, heavy, and self-lubricating. The Texas Lignumvitae, as some call Guayacan, is sometimes used for fence posts and tool handles, but because of its small stature it is of little commercial value. The heartwood is dark greenish brown and takes on a nice finish.

AMERICAN SMOKE TREE

Cotinus obovatus.
Chittamwood.
A low shrubby plant or small tree seldom over 25 feet with an open rounded crown.

Leaves — Deciduous, oval, 2-6 inches long, 2-3 inches wide, rounded or slightly notched at the tip; light purple, often pubescent underneath when young, turning olive green with a paler underside with age; leaves borne on a purple or reddish petiole.

Flowers — Male and female flowers usually on separate trees, greenish yellow, large open feathery clusters with few flowers; pedicels turn purplish.

Fruit — Very small, light brown, oblong or kidney-shaped; borne on slender hairy stalks.

Twigs — Smooth, green or sometimes reddish turning gray with age.

Bark — Furrowed, broken into thin scales; gray to black.

269

The American Smoke Tree is quite rare in the mountains of Alabama, Tennessee, Missouri, and on southwest to Oklahoma and Texas. In Texas, this tree is found in a relatively small number of populations scattered on limestone hills and river bluffs on the Edwards Plateau and North Central Texas. The Smoke Tree is so-named for its showy bloom. The flowers are loose and airy, extending above the leaves. These are borne on slightly fuzzy, purplish stalks which from a distance give the appearance of haze or smoke rising above the tree. This tree, in the same family as Sumac, has leaves which turn bright shades of yellow, orange, and

scarlet during the fall. A distinguishing characteristic is the rounded or oval leaf with a reddish petiole or leaf stem. The Smoke Tree has yellow to orangish-yellow wood which is soft but durable. A yellow dye can be extracted from it and was done so extensively during the Civil War. The American Smoke Tree is one of two species in the genus *Cotinus* existing worldwide. The European species, *Cotinus coggygria*, sometimes called Old World Wig Tree, has showier blooms and is widely planted as an ornamental in the eastern U.S. It does, however, lack the good fall color of the American species.

This tree and Gum Bumelia are often called Chittamwood, which is a reference to a Biblical tree (Shittamwood) and has been loosely applied to several American tree species.

270

CHINESE PISTACHE

Pistacia chinensis.
Medium sized tree about 40 feet tall with a broad, rounded crown forming an equal spread. Trunk short and somewhat stout to 2 feet in diameter.

Leaves — Alternate, evenly pinnate, deciduous about 10-16 inches in length consisting of 10 or more shiny bright-green leaflets 2-4 inches long, turning bright yellow or red in the fall.

Flowers — In spring, branched clusters of small greenish flowers without petals borne from the leaf axils. Male and female flowers appear on separate trees.

271

Fruit — Only from female trees, ¼-inch-long red drupes turning dark blue as they mature in the fall, inedible.

Twigs — Moderately stout, tan to light brown with prominent raised lenticels, scaly terminal bud about ⅓ inch long, pith white.

Bark — Light brown with lighter splotches at first, soon separating into brown flattened ridges and broad light brown fissures, these narrowing and the ridges becoming scaly often breaking into shaggy flakes, eventually turning dark gray, gray, or gray brown with irregular scales.

Chinese Pistache was introduced from China as an ornamental tree for drier areas and as grafting rootstock for commercial Pistachio (*Pistacia vera*) production. In Texas, it has become popular as an ornamental and has become naturalized to a certain extent. It grows rapidly, is remarkably free of pests and disease, drought resistant, and provides brilliant fall color to areas which are otherwise without it. Young trees look awkward but they eventually develop a nice symmetrical rounded crown. The young shoots can be eaten as a vegetable. Some birds eat the fruits, and escaped trees are often found growing under power lines or along fences.

272

TEXAS PISTACHE. *Pistacia texana.*

Large shrub or small tree with several trunks to about 30 feet tall. This plant is found growing naturally only along cliffs near the junction of the Rio Grande and Pecos rivers in Texas and also into northern Mexico. It has relatively small (about 2-4 inches long) shiny, evergreen (in most winters), pinnate leaves that are bronze colored at the growing tip. The leaves are made up of 9 to 19 leaflets roughly ½ to 1 inch in length. In spring, with or before the leaves appear, the flowers are borne in densely-flowered, small lateral branches. The sexes are on separate trees. Small

single-seeded fruits, oval and somewhat flattened, about ¼ inch long, are red at first but turn dark blue or black at maturity. Texas Pistache has been offered as an ornamental shrub for dry landscapes because it is disease free, grows fast, and is drought hardy, but it can be ungainly unless trained when young.

An attractive Texas Pistache can be seen at the Judge Roy Bean Visitor Center in Langtry. The national champion Texas Pistache is 39 feet tall, 51 inches in trunk circumference, and has a crown spread of 46 feet. It is located in the Amistad Recreation Area, run by the National Park Service, near Del Rio.

273

SHINING SUMAC

Rhus copallina.
Flameleaf Sumac.
A small tree to 25 feet, or more commonly a clump-forming shrub found on fence rows, fields, and bottomlands of East and East Central Texas.

Leaves — Compound, alternate, 10-20 small leaflets, green and glossy above, somewhat fuzzy beneath. Leaf rachis winged (having membranous or leaf outgrowth from the leaf branch).

Flowers — Very small, pale green or whitish, borne in terminal clusters. Male and female flowers on separate trees. Blooms in July.

Fruit — Clusters of small red fruit covered with minute hairs. Very acid tasting. The fruit remains on the branch after the leaves have fallen.

274

Twigs — New growth covered with velvety, reddish brown hairs.

Bark — Smooth, white or grayish, often with horizontal markings, sometimes light brown.

The Sumac is quickly recognized in autumn by its bright shades of scarlet and orange. Not only is the leaf color noticeable but also the clusters of bright red fruit which appear in summer and cling on the branch tips until winter. Since the male and female flowers are borne on separate trees, only those trees with female flowers have fruit. The fruit is relished by many species of birds, particularly quail, and a number of mammals. The twigs and leaves are often browsed by white-tailed deer. A refreshing and acidic beverage, sometimes called sumac-ade, can be made by steeping the fruit in boiling water. It is of note that although this plant is in the same family as Poison Ivy and Poison Sumac, it is not irritating. A general rule of thumb is that sumac species with red fruits are safe but those with white fruits (Poison Sumac and Poison Ivy) are to be avoided.

The Sumac wood is soft, light, and coarse grained. The bark, leaves, and fruit are all high in tannin and have been used to cure leather and to produce brown to black dyes. The Sumac is fast growing but short-lived. Although this

275

plant is attractive and has landscape potential, many do not appreciate that it often spreads by root-suckers. The Flameleaf Sumac of Central Texas, however, can often be seen as a single-trunked, nonsuckering tree.

FLAMELEAF SUMAC. *Rhus lanceolata.*
Prairie Flameleaf.

Large shrub or small tree up to 20 feet tall. It was once considered only a variety of Shining Sumac and differs by having narrow leaves up to ½ inch wide and generally having a more western distribution. There has been a recent surge of interest regarding Flameleaf Sumac as cultivated ornamentals for their reliable displays of scarlet fall color; however, some specimens tend to sucker from the roots and form thickets. The national champion Flameleaf Sumac is located in Comal Country and is 29 feet tall, has a trunk circumference of 45 inches, and covers an area 23 feet across.

SMOOTH SUMAC. *Rhus glabra.*
Shumac.

Thicket-forming shrub or small tree to about 15 feet tall found along roadsides and the edge of woods throughout East Texas west to Comanche and Coryell counties. It differs from other sumacs by having smooth, often bluish-white, stems and leaf stalks. The sour fruits can be used to make the refreshing "Sumac-ade" drink and the Indians utilized the dried leaves as a tobacco substitute. Wildlife use the thickets for cover and the abundant fruits provide good winter bird food. Honeybees swarm the large late spring–early summer flower clusters, producing an amber-colored, heavy-bodied honey with a fine flavor. The wood is especially attractive with a bright white sapwood and a green heartwood surrounding a large pith. Smooth Sumac is a good ornamental for areas where its suckering habit is not a problem. It is one of the few trees that reliably give a brilliant scarlet fall color display.

POISON SUMAC. *Rhus vernix.*

Small solitary tree about 15 feet tall, distinguished from the other sumacs by having leaves with smooth margins and white fruits. It is found along seeps and bogs in the East Texas Piney Woods. Some people consider this to be more virulent than its cousin, Poison Ivy. Whatever the case may be, it is capable of inflicting the same discomfort to the un-aware who are susceptible. Fortunately, it frequents areas that are rarely traveled by the public although there are a number of plants in the Boykin Springs State Recreational Area. People often collect the bright red fall leaves, only to discover later it was a terrible mistake as the plant is poisonous throughout the year.

EASTERN BLACK WALNUT

Juglans nigra.
A large deciduous tree to more than 80 feet tall with a round-topped crown and a straight tapering trunk 3 feet in diameter.

Leaves — Alternate, 1-2 feet long, compound with 11-23 thin leaflets 3-5 inches long and about 1 inch in width, light green and smooth above, pale and somewhat downy below, turning yellow in the fall.

Flowers—In the spring, male and female flowers on the same tree, often on the same branch. Male flowers are in stout unbranched catkins 2-5 inches long; female flowers are about ¼ inch long in spikes or in groups of 2-5.

Fruit—Ripening in the fall, usually in clusters of two or three. A smooth round husk 1½ to 2½ inches in diameter, enclosing a hard, roughly-corrugated nut. The nut meat is sweet and edible but somewhat oily. The husk does not split when ripe.

Twigs—Covered with brown fuzz when young but becoming smooth later, leaf scars large and shield shaped, terminal bud blunt, fuzzy gray about ¼ inch long. Pith buff colored and distinctly chambered.

Bark — Dark and smooth when young, becoming brown to black and 2-3 inches thick on older trunks with deep furrows and rounded interlacing ridges.

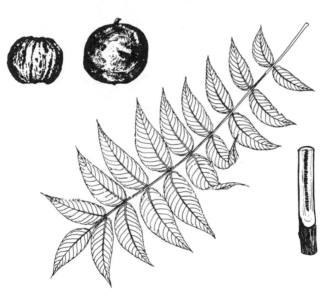

Black Walnut is usually found on deep soils in bottomland floodplains, at the edge of fields, and along streams throughout East and Central Texas west to about Bexar, Goliad, Bosque, and Collin counties, and along the Red River to Hardeman County. Some outlying populations occur in

Bandera and Burnet counties. Black Walnuts usually exist as scattered individuals and are generally considered intolerant of shade. The wood has a whitish sapwood and a chocolate or purple-brown heartwood, which is unique among commercial hardwoods of the United States. It has distinct growth rings, a mild characteristic odor, and is rated one of the finest domestic cabinet woods. Walnut is prized for veneer and furniture construction and is one of the preferred woods for gunstocks. It is strong, hard, shock reisistant, has good texture and finishing properties, and does not shrink or warp with age.

Walnuts have ornamental potential because of their graceful appearance, fast growth rate, and lack of serious insect pests or diseases, They are also relatively drought hardy and the thick bark resists damage. On the other hand, Walnut is difficult to transplant because of the long taproot, the leaves come out late in the spring and drop early in the fall, the nuts can clutter the yard, and the husks contain an indelible brown stain. Walnut roots secrete a substance known as "juglone" which inhibits the growth of some plant species such as fruit trees and tomatoes. Many horticultural varieties have been developed based mainly on larger, thinner-walled fruits. The nuts are a favorite food of squirrels which are largely responsible for dispersing the heavy seeds. It has been said that green Walnut fruits can be used in survival emergencies in much the same way as Buckeye—to stun fish in slow-moving waters. The husks yield a rich brown dye and because of the high tannic acid content do not require a mordant (setting agent). It is also useful for staining wool and leather.

ARIZONA WALNUT. *Juglans major.*
Nogal Silvestre.

Medium sized tree to about 45 feet tall with a trunk 18 inches in diameter. Differs from Eastern Black Walnut by having fewer number of leaflets (usually less than 15), smaller fruits, 1 to 1½ inch wide, and a more westerly range, being found along streams and canyons in Central and West Texas. The wood has the same desirable qualities as Black Walnut and the fruits are a valuable wildlife food.

TEXAS WALNUT. *Juglans microcarpa.*
Little Walnut, Nogal.

Not everything named "Texas" is the biggest. This small tree to about 30 feet tall with a trunk 18 inches in diameter is just a miniature version of its relatives. The leaflets are small, ½ to 1 inch wide, and are strongly scented when bruised. Young plants look somewhat like sumacs. The fruit is usually less than 1 inch wide. It is found scattered in dry rocky ravines and along streams in Central, South, and West Texas. Where the range overlaps with Arizona Walnut they often hybridize, making positive identification difficult. The wood is as desirable as other native Walnuts but the trees seldom reach a productive size. Indians used the Texas Walnut for spears and later settlers used the durable wood for fence posts. The fruits are eaten by wildlife, especially rodents; javelinas are quite fond of them. The national champion Texas Walnut is located in Denton County. It is 160 inches in circumference, 50 feet tall, and has a crown spread of 80 feet.

PECAN

Carya illinoensis.
Large deciduous tree over 100 feet tall with a broadly rounded crown open at the top and a thick straight trunk 4 feet in diameter.

Leaves — Alternate, compound, 12-20 inches long with 9-17 leaflets that are 3-8 inches long and 1-2 inches wide. On top they are smooth to slightly hairy and dark yellow green, slightly paler beneath.

Flowers — In spring, both sexes on the same tree. Male catkins 5-6 inches long, female flowers in short terminal spikes.

Fruit — Ripening in the fall, in clusters of 3-11. The husk is thin and splits into four sections and often stays on the tree

282

after the nut has fallen. The nut is light reddish brown with irregular black or darker brown blotches. The meat is edible, sweet and oily.

Twigs — Stout reddish brown and hairy, terminal bud almost ½ inch long, flattened and pointed at the tip. Lateral buds smaller, hairy, broadly cone-shaped and pointy. Leaf scars are three-lobed and prominent.

Bark — Thick, light brown to reddish brown, with narrow irregular fissures, flattened and scaly.

Pecan is usually found in the deep rich soils associated with streams and river bottoms in East and Central Texas but has been widely planted across the state outside its natural range. Pecan wood has a light reddish-brown sapwood and a darker heartwood. It is not as strong as other hickories and is used primarily for flooring and veneer for paneling and furniture. This is the largest and fastest growing hickory and has become widely cultivated outside of its natural range for the nutrient-rich nuts. It is relatively free of serious pests and diseases but is hard to transplant because of the long taproot. Webworms can be a problem on some trees. The nuts were a favorite food of the Indians and are an important food source for many wildlife species.

Pecans used to be so abundant that large trees were often cut down to harvest a single nut crop. This short-sighted, wasteful practice illlustrates how some of Texas' virgin forests were exploited for profit. The leaves and bark have been used medicinally as an astringent. It is rumored that the high tannic acid content of the leaves inhibits growth of some plants beneath the trees. Pecan is the state tree of Texas. The state champion Pecan is located in Franklin County and is 111 inches in circumference, 115 feet tall, and has a crown spread of 66 feet.

WATER HICKORY. *Carya aquatica.*
Bitter Pecan.

Usually a small tree but reaching heights of 100 feet; differs from Pecan by having fewer numbers of leaflets (7-13) and a round flattened nut with a bitter meat. It is found growing along creek and river bottoms that are occasionally flooded in the southern half of the East Texas Piney Woods. Water Hickory tends to be one of the last trees to leaf out in the spring. This enables it to withstand the spring floods because it is dormant during times of standing water. The national champion Water Hickory can be found at the Longhorn Army Ammunition Depot near Marshall in Harrison County. It is 113 feet tall, with a crown spread of 76 feet and a trunk girth of 133 inches.

NUTMEG HICKORY. *Carya myristicaeformis.*

A somewhat rare tree to about 100 feet, usually found in river bottoms mostly in East Texas with a reported population in Kerr County. It has 5-9 leaflets, and a small rounded nut that is about the same size and shape of the true nutmeg fruit. Mature trees have a shaggy bark that resembles Shagbark Hickory (*Carya ovata*) but is broken into thinner strips. This is our only native hickory with silvery scales

covering the lower leaf surfaces, the winter twigs, and buds. Nutmeg Hickory and Durand Oak are considered by some to be relics of an earlier age because they have very similar spotty distributions.

BITTERNUT HICKORY

Carya cordiformis.
A deciduous tree to 100 feet tall with spreading or ascending branches forming a narrow crown rounded at the top and a straight trunk about 2 feet in diameter.

Leaves — Alternate, compound 6-10 inches long usually with 7-9 leaflets but may have as few as 5 or as many as 11. The terminal leaflets are 4-6 inches in length and 1 to 1½ inches across the middle. They are firm and thin, shiny green on the top surface and lighter green and slightly hairy on the underside.

Flowers — In spring, males on slender hairy catkins and females single or paired on short spikes at the ends of the branchlets.

Fruit — Ripening in the fall, nearly round or slightly tapered about 1 inch long, the thin husk is covered with fine yellow hairs. The nut is reddish to gray brown and contains a bitter kernel.

Twigs — Slender green at first and minutely hairy, later turning brownish, often yellow glandular and hairy near the tips with large lighter colored, heart-shaped leaf scars. The most distinctive aspect of the tree is the ½-inch-long, sulfur-yellow, terminal bud which does not have covering scales, allowing the tiny folds of the first leaves to be seen.

Bark — On young trees it is smooth and unbroken, gray brown or gray; on older trunks it is tight and hard with shallow furrows and close, flat interlacing ridges.

Bitternut Hickory is usually found in moist areas along streams and river bottoms throughout East Texas from the eastern part of Lamar County southwest to eastern Milam and Washington counties. There are also isolated populations located in Dallas and Colorado counties. It is generally intolerant of shade but at least on bottomlands tolerates competition as well as most of its associated species.

Bitternut is one of the fastest growing hickories but forms a deep taproot early in life and is consequently difficult to transplant. The wood has most of the desirable qualities of other hickories but it is somewhat lighter and considered inferior to Shagbark or Mockernut material. The meat of the nut is so bitter even squirrels rarely eat them but an oil extracted from it was used in the treatment of rheumatism. This is probably the most widespread and uniformly distributed hickory species in North America but in Texas it is mainly confined to the eastern part of the state.

287

SHAGBARK HICKORY

Carya ovata.
Shellbark Hickory.
Picturesque tree to 100 feet tall with a narrow but somewhat spreading crown and a straight trunk 18 inches in diameter.

Leaves—Deciduous, alternate, compound, 8 to 15 inches long. Leaflets usually 5 (rarely 7), the terminal usually the largest, 5 to 7 inches in length and 2 to 3 inches wide with toothed margins that bear a minute tuft of hair on each tooth. The leaves have a pleasingly pungent odor when bruised.

Flowers — In spring, the male and female parts separate but on the same tree. Male catkins slender and hairy, 4 to 5 inches long, the female flowers on short terminal spikes.

Fruit — Ripening in the fall, nearly round with a smooth, four-ribbed, hard light-brown shell. One to 2½ inches in diameter, the husk ¼ to ½ inch thick separating into four sections.

Twigs — Brown and shiny at first, turning gray with age, marked with prominent leaf scars and the pith star-shaped in cross section. Terminal bud about ¾ inch long with persistent outer scales.

Bark — Smooth and firm when young, becoming somewhat darker and breaking into narrow loose plates that are attached near the middle and curve out from the trunk giving it a distinctive shaggy appearance.

Shagbark Hickory is frequently found in rich woods, bottomlands, and along streams in the Piney Woods of East Texas. It is often found in the understory of young forests as it is very shade-tolerant when young. Over a period of time Shagbark Hickory will become one of the components in the Oak-Hickory climax forest potentially covering a large portion of the East Texas Piney Woods. The wood has a whitish sapwood and a brownish heartwood, is very hard and heavy, and is well known for its strength and shock resistance. These qualities made Shagbark Hickory ideal for hammers, axes, tools, sledges, and formerly for wagon-wheel spokes.

Hickory wood makes good fuel and is popular for smoking meats. This hickory grows slowly and develops a long taproot making it difficult to transplant. Shagbark nuts are very tasty and are the commercial hickory nuts relished by many. Most of the horticultural varieties are based on nut size and shell thickness. The nuts are eaten by squirrels, and the eastern Indians fermented them into a drink called *powcohiccora,* which is where the name "hickory" comes from. The state champion Shagbark Hickory is located in Sabine National Forest. It is 85 inches in circumference, 120 feet tall, and has a crown spread of 55 feet.

SWAMP HICKORY. *Carya leiodermis.*

Swamp Hickory differs from Shagbark by usually having 7 leaflets and tight bark that is not shaggy. It is found in bottomlands and swamps of East Texas.

MOCKERNUT HICKORY

Carya tomentosa.
A handsome tree to about 100 feet tall with an oblong to broadly rounded crown and a straight trunk 2 feet in diameter.

Leaves — Alternate, deciduous, having a spicy odor when crushed, compound, 8-16 inches in length with 5-9 leaflets, the upper ones ranging from 4-8 inches long and 3-5 inches wide.

Flowers — In spring, the male flowers in light green catkins 4-6 inches long, female flowers on short spikes at the ends of the branches.

291

Fruit—Heavy, round or egg-shaped, 1½ to 3 inches across with the thick husk splitting to expose the hard thick-shelled nut with a sweet edible kernel.

Twigs—Stout and rigid, reddish brown and hairy when young, becoming smooth later. The terminal bud more than ½ inch long and ½ inch across at the base, leaf scars large and three-lobed.

Bark — Dark gray and relatively thin with a crisscross or net pattern of shallow furrows and flat narrow ridges.

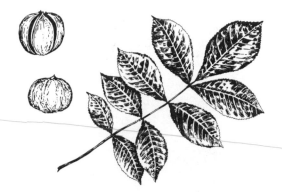

Mockernut Hickory is relatively common throughout the pine forests of East Texas west to Lamar and eastern Travis County. It is usually found in moist upland sites or along creeks and streams as a climax species under the faster, shorter-lived trees. The wood is comparable to that of Shagbark Hickory and is especially good for tool handles because of its shock resistance and resiliency.

This is a slow growing tree that quickly develops a deep taproot, making it difficult to transplant. Few diseases bother Mockernut, but twig girdler insects often disfigure young trees by cutting off the branch ends or, worse, by removing the terminal leader. The heavy nuts are tasty but hardly worth the effort needed to extract them from their hard thick shell. They can be soaked in water and used without the husk in fires to give food a hickory-smoked flavor. The state champion Mockernut Hickory is 115 feet tall, has a trunk circumference of 105 inches, and shades an area 66 feet across. It is located on the Alabama-Coushatta Indian Reservation near Livingston.

292

BLACK HICKORY

Carya texana.
Texas Hickory.
Medium sized deciduous tree occasionally to 100 feet tall, with short crooked branches forming a narrow or spreading crown and a trunk diameter of two feet.

Leaves — Alternate, compound, to 12 inches in length, the terminal leaflet about 5 inches long and 2 inches wide. Leaflets thin and firm, most often 7 but sometimes 5, covered with rust-colored hairs on the lower surface when young, becoming smooth with age.
Flowers — In spring, male flowers usually in 3 clustered catkins 2½ to 5 inches long, female flowers 1 or 2 on short spikes at the ends of the branches.

293

Fruit — Almost round, ripening in the fall, 1½ to 2 inches in diameter; the rounded nut inside the thin husk has a thick shell protecting a small sweet kernel.

Twigs — Slender, stiff, reddish brown with rust-colored hairs at first, becoming gray and smooth when older. Leaf scars three-lobed and prominent. Winter buds less than ½ inch long with yellowish-brown loose scales that have a small tuft of whitish hairs at the tip.

Bark — Thick, silver to dark gray when young and almost black on older trees. Deeply furrowed with irregular fissures that form blocky ridges on mature trees.

Black Hickory is usually found on dry sandy uplands and rocky hillsides throughout the eastern part of the state west to the areas of Gillespie and Bexar counties. It is often associated with Blackjack and Post Oak. Mockernut and Black Hickory are quite similar and sometimes mistaken for each other where their ranges overlap. Black Hickory wood is too small to be of commercial value but it is ideal for fuel because it has a nice flame, is virtually sparkless, burns a long time, and leaves a clean ash. The nuts, without the husks, can be used to flavor cooking fires and are a minor food source to squirrels and hogs. This is our most western hickory other than the Pecan.

PIGNUT HICKORY. *Carya glabra.*

Differs from Black Hickory by having usually 5, sometimes 7, leaflets and hairless leaves, twigs, and winter buds. In Texas, it is found only in the East Texas Piney Woods area.

HOPTREE

Ptelea trifoliata.
Wafer Ash.
Shrub or small tree rarely over 20 feet tall with a rounded, loosely-branched crown.

Leaves — Alternate, deciduous, trifoliate, and quite variable. Leaflets up to 6 inches long and 3 inches broad but usually much smaller, margins entire or finely toothed, upper surface dark green and shiny or slightly hairy, lower surface softly pubescent or smooth. Leaves aromatic when crushed and turning yellow in fall.

Flowers — In spring with the new leaves, usually in rounded branched clusters borne near the ends of the branches. Sexes together or on separate flowers in the same cluster. Petals about ⅛ inch long, 4 or 5, greenish white with a characteristic odor.

Fruit — Maturing in late summer but often persisting through the winter. About one inch wide, borne on stalks in terminal clusters, 2-3 red-brown seeds surrounded by a broad papery wing.

Twigs — Slender, softly hairy when young, green at first but quickly turning red brown, odorous when scratched. Winter buds very small, yellowish and woolly, lacking a true terminal bud. Older twigs and branchlets with prominent lenticels and light splotches.

Bark — Quite variable but usually red brown and smooth and tight at first, with light-colored splotches turning silver, gray brown, or brown, and finally becoming roughened with flakes peeling at the edges or with long flat ridges with shallow fissures.

Hoptree is scattered throughout East and Central Texas but is perhaps most abundant in the Edwards Plateau region where it occurs on all but the wettest or driest sites. It is usually an understory plant but is often found growing at the edges of woods or along creek drainages. The wood is heavy, hard, and attractive with a close grain but rarely grows big enough for anything but novelty uses. Early settlers, desperate for a drink, substituted the fruits for true hops in beer-making, giving rise to the current common name.

Hoptree, a member of the citrus family, is also known as skunk bush by some because of the distinctive odor emitted when the leaves are crushed.

This plant has ornamental potential, and several cultivars have been developed, based mainly on leaf color. The attractive light green fruit give a good effect against the handsome glossy foliage. Hoptree also has dependable fall color. Medicinally, the aromatic bark and roots have been used as a substitute for quinine, a remedy for dyspepsia, and as a mild tonic to promote the appetite.

HERCULES CLUB

Zanthoxylum clava-herculis.
Prickly Ash, Toothache Tree, Pepper-
wood, Tear-Blanket, Wait-A-Bit.
Small tree to 30 feet tall with a low
rounded crown and a short trunk.

Leaves — Alternate, deciduous, once pinnate with 7-15 leaflets
often with one or two black prickles at the base or remotely spaced along the central leafstalk, 5 to 8 inches
in length. Leaflets 1 to 2½ inches long, glossy green above,
somewhat paler beneath.

Flowers — In spring as branching elongated clusters of greenish ⅛ to ¼ inch across, five-petaled flowers terminating
the branches. The sexes are usually found on separate
trees.

Fruit — Maturing in summer, small dry fruits split open to expose a shiny black seed about ⅓ inch long.

Twigs — Somewhat stout to slender, gray or brown, moder-

298

ately hairy at first, becoming smooth. Armed with stout dark-colored prickles.

Bark — Gray and usually covered with prickle-tipped, broadly conical, corky growths that often eventually cover the lower part of the trunk until it becomes a series of corky ridges and deep furrows.

Hercules Club is most common along fence lines but is also found in pine forests and at the edge of openings in the eastern fourth of the state. It is intolerant of shade and rarely found as an understory member. The genus name refers to its yellow wood which is soft and weak. The common name Hercules Club comes from the warclub-like appearance given by the knobby warts on the trunk. The bark and leaves, when chewed, produce a peculiar numbing effect on the inside of the mouth. Indians and early settlers alike used this plant to deaden the pain of toothaches; it was also used as a wash to soothe itching skin. A decoction of the bark was formerly used to aid certain stomach problems such as flatulence, poor digestion, and diarrhea. Both the bark and fruit have been used to treat rheumatism. A pepper substitute can be made from finely ground portions of the bark. Other than birds, few species of wildlife utilize this plant. Passing through a birds' digestive system helps the seed germinate better, which explains why these trees seem to proliferate along fence lines. The state champion Hercules Club is located on the Alabama-Coushatta Indian

Reservation, near Livingston in Polk County. It is 50 feet tall and has a crown spread of 32 feet and a trunk circumference of 31 inches.

TOOTHACHE TREE. *Zanthoxylum hirsutum.* Lime Prickly Ash.

A prickly shrub or small tree seldom to 20 feet tall found from North Central to South Texas at the edge of woods, along fence lines, or in mixed brush. It differs from Hercules Club by usually having only 5 leaflets and smaller plant parts in general. The leaves and bark of this plant have the same numbing properties as other *Zanthoxylum* species.

COLIMA. *Zanthoxylum fagara.*

A prickly evergreen shrub or small tree growing up to 30 feet found in South Texas and near the coast in Southeast Texas. It is prevalent in the Lower Rio Grande Valley. Colima differs from the other *Zanthoxylum* spp. by having a winged-leaf rachis and leaflets that are oval to obovate and smaller in size.

TREE OF HEAVEN

Ailanthus altissima.
Ghetto Palm.
A medium sized tree 30-40 feet with a graceful oval crown and a trunk 1½ feet thick or suckering from the roots forming a thicket.

Leaves — Emerging mid spring, alternate, odd single pinnately compound, deciduous, 1 to over 3 feet in length with 13 to 25 stalked leaflets 3-5 inches long and coarsely 2-4 toothed, each tooth having a distinctive visible nectary gland at the base. Leaflets are dull yellowish green above and usually glaucous below. The leaves have a characteristic strong odor when crushed and the young growth is a deep reddish bronze.

301

Flowers — Appearing in mid to late spring, the sexes usually on separate trees as small clusters of tiny five-petaled flowers in loose, terminal panicles up to 1 foot long. The male flowers have 10 stamens and emit a strong odor most people find unpleasant.

Fruit — Two winged flattened seeds that overall resemble little twisted propellers, two inches long, green or yellowish at first, maturing in the fall to reddish brown.

Twigs — Thick and stout, dull yellowish brown with very little secondary branching and a large reddish orange pith.

Bark — Smooth and green when young, becoming thin, gray, and slightly roughened with age.

Tree of Heaven is a native of western China. Introduced originally as an ornamental, it has spread almost everywhere throughout the contiguous United States, becoming a pesky weed. In the wild it is found on a variety of sites across the eastern two thirds of Texas along clearings, forest openings, and at the edge of woods where it often forms thickets almost resembling smooth sumac or bamboo. In the city it frequents vacant lots and fence lines. Few trees are as rugged as the *Ailanthus,* which has become famous for surviving high stress situations in the harshest urban environments. (This was the tree that inspired Betty Smith's novel *A Tree Grows in Brooklyn.*) The long compound leaves give a decided tropical effect, the fast growth rate is almost fantastic, and the graceful open growth form is quite attractive. Like pigeons that have adapted too well to city life, however, they are now held in low esteem and are rarely seen in the nursery trade. Tree of Heaven is not without virtue as it is one of the best tall tree species that can be recommended for planting in areas cursed by Texas cotton root rot.

WESTERN SOAPBERRY

Sapindus drummondii.
Jaboncillo.
Small to medium sized tree about 30 or more feet in height with a rounded crown at maturity and a trunk to 2 feet thick.

Leaves — Alternate, deciduous, up to 18 inches in length. The 4-19 leaflets alternate along the central leafstalk, giving the leaf an even pinnate compound appearance. Leaflets yellow green, 1½ to 4 inches in length turning yellow in fall.

303

Flowers — In spring to early summer as elongated branched clusters, 6-9 inches in length, five-petaled flowers less than ¼ inch across.

Fruit — In terminal branched clusters ripening in the fall and persisting most of the winter. Round, smooth, amber, and translucent leathery about ½ inch in diameter. Turning black and wrinkled in late winter. Each fruit containing a single, hard, dark-brown seed about ¼ inch in diameter.

Twigs — Somewhat slender to moderately stout, yellow-green to gray, no true terminal bud, axillary buds superposed.

Bark — Gray, tan, or reddish brown, roughened at first but eventually peeling off in thin flakes.

Western Soapberry is found throughout Texas along streams, fences, and at the edge of woods. This nearly ubiquitous native range led the Texas Department of Agriculture to pronounce this *the* tree for Texas landscaping (not to be confused with the official state tree—Pecan). As a landscape plant, Soapberry is moderately fast growing, tolerates poor sites, has reliable yellow fall color, and has few insect or disease problems. On the other hand, it is moderately short-lived, has poisonous fruits, and often forms thickets. Although the fruits are poison, they were useful to the Indians and early settlers; they contain up to 37 percent saponin and readily form a lather when macerated in water. They were widely used as a shampoo and for washing clothes, a practice that still persists in Mexico. Although they cause a skin irritation to some people, the fruits were used in folk medicine to suppress fevers and to treat some kidney disorders.

The hard round seeds have been used to make rosaries, necklaces, and as buttons. The flower nectar is believed to be poisonous and the fruit is rarely eaten by animals. Indians supposedly used the fruit much like rotenone to capture fish after they had been stunned. The yellowish wood of Soapberry is hard and close grained but splits readily along the rings when pounded. This quality made it popular for making baskets and packsaddle frames. The national champion Western Soapberry is 62 feet tall and has a trunk circumference of 82 inches and a crown spread of 55 feet. It is located in Newton County.

MEXICAN BUCKEYE

Ungnadia speciosa.
Irregular-shaped shrub or small tree with several, often leaning, trunks up to 20 feet tall and 6 inches in diameter.

Leaves — Alternate, deciduous, odd - pinnately compound up to 1 foot in length with 5 to 7 (occasionally 3) leaflets about 3 to 5 inches long and about half as wide. Dark green and shiny on top, paler and somewhat hairy below, turning yellow in the fall before dropping.

Flowers — In early spring before or with the unfolding leaves, as small clusters of showy pink 4 to 5 parted flowers, both sexes present in the same flowers, with 7 to 10 exerted pink stamens and a single pistil. Individual flowers about 1 inch across.

Fruit — Maturing in early fall as hanging, three-lobed, woody capsules about 2 inches across containing as many as three hard round seeds up to 1 inch in diameter. Pods often persisting on the plant for up to 2 years. Seeds are dark brown to almost black, shiny and with a large white "eye" that gives it the appearance of a true buckeye (*Aesculus* sp.)

Twigs — Slender to moderately stout, reddish brown and slightly hairy at first, becoming smooth with age. No true terminal bud; the axillary buds are round, reddish brown and scaly. Smaller flower buds can often be found flanking the leaf buds. Leaf scars are relatively large and elongate.

Bark — Brown, thin, and smooth, becoming gray with slight scaly ridges and shallow furrows at maturity.

Mexican Buckeye is not a member of the true Buckeye family but the seeds look somewhat similar to those of certain *Aesculus* species such as Texas Buckeye *(Aesculus arguta)*. It is usually found in fairly alkaline soil along creeks, draws, and canyons in Central, South, and Trans-Pecos Texas. Populations occur as far east as Harris County and extend northward to Collin County. Individuals from northern populations tend to be slightly smaller in stature, bushier, have smaller leaves and fruits, and are more cold-hardy than plants from southern locations.

Bees make an excellent honey from the flowers and the hard round seeds were often used by kids in rural areas as a substitute for store-bought marbles. One or two of the sweet seeds can be eaten without discomfort but they are otherwise considered poisonous, causing vomiting and other unpleasantries.

From a distance, a Mexican Buckeye covered with its early spring pink flowers can easily be mistaken for a Redbud or Peach tree, both of which bloom at roughly the same time. This is one of the more attractive native plants that has, until recently, received little attention as an ornamental. The showy early spring flowers, good yellow fall color, and the peculiar persistent fruits make this a distinctive plant the year round.

CHINABERRY

Melia azedarach.
Pride of China.
Medium sized tree about 40 feet tall with a rounded wide-branching crown and a trunk to 1½ feet thick.

Leaves — Alternate, deciduous, odd bipinnately compound, each leaflet 1 to 2 inches long and about half as wide, smooth on both surfaces, light green at first, becoming shiny dark green when mature and turning yellow in fall.
Flowers — Appearing with the unfolding leaves in mid to late spring as branched clusters up to 10 inches long with ½-inch fragrant flowers. Each perfect flower has 5 lilac-

colored petals somewhat curled back with a single pistil and 10 dark purple stamens clustered together.

Fruit — Usually abundant, ripening in the fall but often persisting through the winter. Because they begin forming from the early spring terminal flower clusters, the mature fruit is found at the branch base. The fruits are borne in drooping clusters of rounded berries ½ to ¾ inch in diameter. Hard and green at first, becoming yellow and soft when mature. The bitter pulp is poisonous to people and pigs.

Twigs — Stout and somewhat pithy with prominent leaf scars and rounded, gray, suede-textured buds, green and smooth with white lenticels when young, turning orange to brown with age.

Bark — Dark green, thin, smooth and tight at first, becoming dark steel gray with distinctive thick, often flat-topped, ridges when mature.

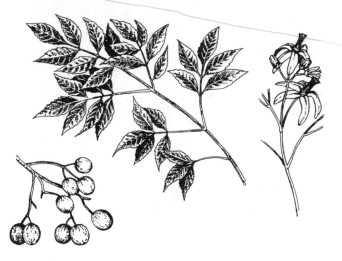

Chinaberry is a legendary tree worshipped for as long as man can remember in the temples of Persia, Malaya, and Ceylon. It is native from Syria through Southeast Asia but has been widely cultivated and has naturalized throughout mild climates. In Texas it can be found across the eastern half of the state on all but the wettest or driest sites. It was originally introduced as a street or shade tree where it gained appreciation for its fast growth and dense shade. Today, Chinaberry is considered a pesky weed tree because of its relatively short life span, weak wood, and tendency to reseed everywhere.

Chinaberry is a member of the Mahogany family and the attractive wood is used for cabinetmaking in its homeland but generates little interest here. The green fruits are favored by kids for throwing or slingshot ammo. Ripe fruits are poisonous and are said to contain a narcotic alkaloid but the pulp oil and seeds have been used to eliminate intestinal worms. If horses eat the berries they are supposed to be protected from botfly attacks, and a decoction of the fruits can be sprinkled on other plants as an organic insecticide against cutworms and other insects. Berries have been used as a substitute for mothballs and also packed with dried fruit to prevent insect attacks. The root bark has been used as a purgative, an emetic, and to promote the onset of menstruation. Chinaberry leaves have been used to treat hysteria, and the tree exudes a gum considered by some to have aphrodisiac qualities. Cattle can eat the profuse fruit apparently without ill effects, and several well known songbirds such as mockingbirds and robins gorge themselves until they become temporarily dazed and confused. Supposedly, Chinaberry was introduced into western cultivation from Greek monasteries where the dried seeds were used as rosary beads.

UMBRELLA TREE. *Melia azedarach* f. *umbraculifera.*

Umbrella tree is a mutation of the species that has become a popular ornamental. It was originally found near the San Jacinto battlefield in 1894 and is readily recognized by its distinctive low umbrella-shaped crown. This is a good shade tree for urban areas as it is fast growing, relatively pest free, casts a dense shade, and besides the attractive growth form, the broad crown rarely reaches 30 feet in height which keeps the tree out of most powerlines.

Araliaceae - Ginseng Family

DEVIL'S WALKING STICK

Aralia spinosa.
Hercules Club.
Peculiar looking small tree to about
30 feet tall, sometimes branching to
form a flattened crown but often only
a single spiny polelike trunk topped by an umbrella
of large leaves.

Leaves — Deciduous, twice pinnate, up to 4 feet long and 3 feet
wide. Leaflets numerous, 1 to 4 inches in length, dark
green above, paler below, the leaf stalks usually armed
with small spines. Turning bronze red and yellow in
autumn.
Flowers — In mid to late summer as large (one foot or more
across) and rounded branched clusters of small, light yellow or white, five-petaled flowers about ⅛ inch wide.

Fruit — Ripening in the fall, wine red, purple, to black, about ⅛ inch in diameter angled with 3 to 5 sides, very juicy with a single seed about ¹⁄₁₀ inch in diameter.

Twigs — Very thick, light brown, with many stout short prickles, leaf scars somewhat V-shaped reaching at least half way around the twig, pith large and white.

Bark — Dark or light brown to gray, remotely armed with stout prickles, shallowly fissured with wide irregular ridges.

Devil's Walking Stick is a fast growing short-lived plant found near streams and along the edge of woods in the pine forests of East Texas. Occasionally it suckers from the roots to make small thickets. It has definite ornamental possibilities as it is free from pest and disease problems, and the stout stems, large leaves, and immense flower clusters give it a distinct subtropical appearance; however, the stems are easily killed by fire and the thin bark is often damaged by mowing equipment. The bark has some reputed medicinal value and has been used to treat toothaches, rheumatism, and as a stimulant. Although in some areas this tree is called Hercules Club, that name is properly applied to *Zanthoxylum clava - hercules*. The state champion Devil's Walking Stick is 40 feet tall and has a crown spread of 12 feet and a trunk circumference of 14 inches. It is located in the Sabine National Forest in Sabine County.

RED MAPLE

Acer rubrum.
A medium sized deciduous tree to about 80 feet tall with a narrow rounded crown and a 2-foot trunk diameter.

Leaves — Opposite, simple, 2-6 inches in length, three- to five-lobed. Bright green above, pale or whitish beneath, petioles often reddish.

Flowers — Bright red in clusters along young branches before the leaves in early spring.

Fruit — Spring to early summer on slender hanging stalks. Paired samaras with red or yellow wings ½ to 1 inch in length.

314

Twigs — Smooth, usually slender, reddish with dark red buds.
Bark — Gray, thin and smooth at first, later turning into shallow furrows and flat scaly plates or broad ridges.

Red Maple is most common in wet or swampy sites but is also found on drier ridges throughout the Piney Woods area of East Texas. They usually occur as scattered large individuals in the forest, often with a number of young plants in any given area. The wood is similar to that of other soft maples: whitish, straight grained, moderately heavy, and with indistinct rings. It is used for boxes, crates, furniture, and pulp. This is a popular ornamental and shade tree that provides year-round color with a spectacular fall display when the foliage turns bright shades of red, yellow, and orange. Although it grows fast, Red Maple is relatively short-lived and has a shallow root system. The thin bark is easily damaged, and on poor sites the trees tend to be unhealthy. Wildlife enjoy the abundant seeds and the foliage is browsed by deer. Maple syrup can be made from Red Maple but it takes quite a bit more than from Sugar Maple (*Acer sacchurum*) because the sugar content is lower. Red Maple is considered to be one of the most common trees in eastern North America and is the state tree of Rhode Island.

SILVER MAPLE. *Acer saccharinum.*

A medium sized tree native to the northeast but often cultivated in Texas. It differs from Red Maple by having leaves divided into 5 deep lobes, and larger fruits (1½ to three inches in length). Most authorities consider this species to be a poor ornamental choice because of its weak wood, shallow roots, poor performance on dry soils, and relatively short life span.

315

FLORIDA MAPLE

Acer barbatum.
Hard Maple, Southern Sugar Maple.
A medium sized deciduous tree to about 55 feet tall with a rounded crown and a trunk to 2 feet in diameter.

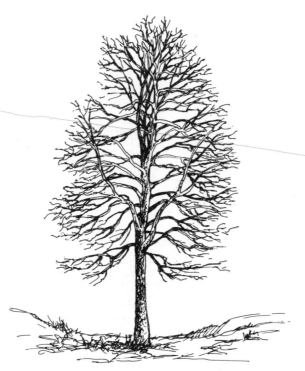

Leaves — Opposite, simple, 1½ to 3½ inches in length, 3 or 5-lobed. Dark green above, somewhat hairy and whitish beneath.
Flowers — Single or bisexual, yellowish green, borne with the leaves on long slender stalks.
Fruit — Early summer, ¾ inch long, green or reddish.
Twigs — Smooth, slender, reddish brown.

316

Bark — Thin, gray, or whitish, becoming somewhat furrowed with age.

Florida Maple is found along streams and in low woodlands in East Texas. It is sometimes planted as an ornamental for its fall foliage colors of yellows and oranges but the thin bark is easily damaged. The sap of Florida Maple can be made into syrup although the sugar content is lower than that of Sugar Maple (*Acer saccharum*). The hard, straight-grained wood is of little commerical value because of the relatively small size of the tree.

SUGAR MAPLE. *Acer saccharum.*
Hard Maple.

Closely related to Florida Maple and is usually considered to be a larger version with bigger leaves (3-8 inches long)

317

and fruits (½ to 1½ inches in length). Sugar Maple is one of the best known and most important trees of eastern North America but in Texas is found only in the northeast forests. The wood is valued for many uses, the tree is important to wildlife, and it is well known for the syrup made from the sap.

CHALK MAPLE. *Acer leucoderme.*

A small tree to about 30 feet tall with light gray to whitish bark. It differs from Florida and Sugar Maples by having dark yellow-green leaves that are softly hairy on the lower surface when mature and a light or chalk-colored bark. It is uncommon in deep East Texas.

BIGTOOTH MAPLE

Acer grandidentatum.
Sugar Maple, Palo De Azucar.
Large deciduous shrub or small tree
to 45 feet tall with an open, rounded
crown and a short trunk to 1 foot in
diameter.

Leaves — Opposite, simple, 2-5 inches long and wide, 3-5 lobed,
occasionally with a few rounded teeth per lobe. Upper
surface dark green and shiny, the lower paler and somewhat hairy.

319

Flowers — Appearing with the leaves in the spring, yellow, on hairy, short-stalked, few-flowered clusters.
Fruit — Late summer to early fall, about 1 inch long, green or slightly reddish with a brown wing.
Twigs — Slender, smooth, red to reddish brown, buds red to reddish brown, pointed at the tip.
Bark — Thin, gray, or light brown, becoming dark brown with age and forming platelike scales.

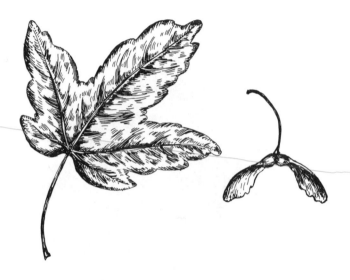

Bigtooth Maple, a close relative of the Sugar Maple, is found in protected canyons, valleys, and along mountain stream banks at elevations of about 4,000 to 6,500 feet in the Trans-Pecos and northern Mexico. It also grows in the Rocky Mountains westward to Idaho. The wood is hard and usually straight grained but of little commerical importance due to its small size and scattered occurrence. It has good ornamental possibilities because of its red and yellow fall foliage and good growth rate, but the thin bark is easily damaged and the tree has a tendency to branch close to the ground forming narrow branch angles. The fruit and foliage are eaten by wildlife and the sap can be made into sugar. Beautiful stands of these maples can be seen in McKittrick Canyon of Guadalupe Mountains National Park and in the Chisos Mountains of Big Bend National Park.

320

UVALDE BIGTOOTH MAPLE. *Acer grandidentatum* var. *sinuosum.*

Differs from the species by having 3 lobes with smooth margins. Together they form the Lost Maples of the Edwards Plateau. These trees were once more abundant during an earlier age when the climate was cooler and more moist, but now remain only in protected cove or canyon areas of the Edwards Plateau, mainly in Bandera, Kendall, and Real counties.

BOX ELDER

Acer negundo.
Medium sized tree to 70 feet tall with a thick spreading crown.

Leaves — Opposite, compound. Leaflets 3-7, 2-5 inches long, light green.
Flowers — Appearing before the leaves in early spring. Very small, yellowish green, sexes on separate trees.
Fruit — Late summer to early fall, in clusters to 8 inches long. Samara 1 to 1½ inches long.
Twigs — Stiff, long, smooth and shiny or pubescent. Green or purplish.
Bark — Smooth, thin, green when young, forming pale gray or brown narrow ridges and small fissures with age.

322

Box Elders often appear as pioneer species wherever water is nearby in East, Central, and South Texas. It can occasionally be found on poorer drier sites. Its versatility, general hardiness, and rapid growth once made Box Elder a popular shade tree around early homesteads and it was frequently used for street and shelterbelt plantings. It has since fallen into disfavor due to its relatively short life span, poor growth form, shallow root system, tendency to sprout prolifically from the trunk, and aggressive nature of reseeding everywhere. The wood is weak and whitish but on freshly cut surfaces is marked with characteristic bright reddish streaks.

Young Box Elders are sometimes confused with Poison Ivy but they are readily distinguished by their opposite leaf arrangement whereas Poison Ivy leaves are arranged alternately. Box Elder seeds are a valuable wildlife food. The sap can be made into syrup but the sugar content is inferior to that of Sugar Maple.

323

RED BUCKEYE

Aesculus pavia.
Early deciduous shrub or small tree
to about 20 feet tall with a rounded
crown.

Leaves — Opposite, with 5 or rarely 7 leaflets. Leaflets 2-6 inches
in length, thin, dark green and shiny above, lighter
beneath.

Flowers — In spring, with the new leaves. Red tubular flowers
about 1 inch long borne on terminal clusters 4-8 inches
long.

Fruit — Rounded, smooth, leathery capsule 1-2 inches across
containing 1-3 large light to dark brown seeds with a
white "eye."

324

Twigs — Thick, round, smooth or finely hairy with large scaly buds and conspicuous lenticels. The terminal inflorescence causes the branches to take on a crooked nature.
Bark — Smooth, tight, thin and gray, becoming somewhat scaly with age.

Red Buckeye is usually an understory plant growing in moist woods and along stream banks throughout the East Texas pine forests and west to Central Texas in the Edwards Plateau. The attractive flowers and foliage, fast growth, and short stature make it a good ornamental shrub. Buckeyes have a somewhat offset life cycle as they leaf out and go dormant earlier than their associates. Consequently, specimen plants—especially in full sun—will begin to shed their leaves in late summer, much to the alarm of the inexperienced gardener. The large heavy seeds are poisonous and only rarely eaten by wildlife. Various parts of the plant including the seeds and buds have been used by Indian groups to stun fish: The seeds are ground up and used as a substance (similar to rotenone) to render the fish unconscious in slow-moving streams or small quiet pools. Buckeye fruit contains aesculin, a compound which is used as a sunscreening agent. The scarlet flowers are often visited by hummingbirds.

325

YELLOW BUCKEYE. *Aesculus pavia* var. *flavescens.*

Confined to the Edwards Plateau and differs from Red Buckeye by having yellow flowers and in general a more western distribution. Where the ranges of the Red and Yellow Buckeye overlap in Central Texas one can see all gradations of these two colors in the flowers.

TEXAS BUCKEYE. *Aesculus arguta.*

A shrub or small tree that is distinguished from other Buckeyes by having 7-11 leaflets, yellow flowers, a spiny capsule, and black seeds. It is found from Northeast to Central and East Texas. The national champion Texas Buckeye is 30 feet tall and has a trunk circumference of 51 inches, and a crown spread of 24 feet. It is growing in Gillespie County.

OHIO BUCKEYE. *Aesculus glabra.*

A small tree to about 20 feet tall found in East Texas. It can be distinguished from other native buckeyes in Texas by having 5-7 leaflets, yellow flowers, and a spiny capsule. This is the state tree of Ohio.

326

FLOWERING DOGWOOD

Cornus florida.
Small graceful tree to about 30 feet tall with horizontal branches turning up at the tips resulting in a flat-topped crown and a layered effect. The short trunk is rarely over 10 inches in diameter.

Leaves — Opposite, simple, deciduous, 2 to 5½ inches in length with a smooth margin, dark green above, paler beneath, the curving leaf veins paralleling the margins, turning various shades of red in fall.

Flowers — In spring before most other trees have leafed out. The tiny greenish-yellow flowers are surrounded by 4 white (rarely pink) showy bracts up to 2½ inches in length.

Fruit — Ripening in the fall and persisting over the winter as tight clusters of red shiny football-shaped drupes about ⅜ inch in length enclosing one or two seeds, inedible and somewhat toxic to humans.

327

Cornaceae - Dogwood Family

Twigs — Slender, light green to yellowish green, reddish, purplish or bluish, often covered with a whitish bloom, vegetative buds composed of two valvate scales. Flower buds terminal and stalked, resembling a flattened sphere with a small point rising from the middle, made up of the four showy bracts that will grow and expand from the base like fingernails.

Bark — Reddish brown to gray brown or black, older trunks with a distinct checkerboard pattern of squared blocks and shallow furrows.

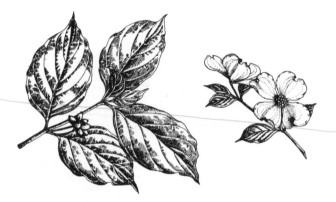

Flowering Dogwood is found in moist woods and along streams as a very shade-tolerant understory tree in the pine forests of East Texas. They are readily recognized in the spring when they cover themselves with upturned flowers, which are really the showy bracts, shining through the leafless woods. With the red fall color of the leaves and bright red fruits held through winter, it is no wonder that Flowering Dogwood is generally considered to be one of our most beautiful native flowering trees.

The wood is hard, close grained, shock resistant (it doesn't broom on the end under impact), and becomes smoother with wear. Most weaving shuttles are still made from Dogwood, but before the age of plastics it was used for a variety of purposes such as pulleys, spindles, mallet heads, mauls, wedges, hay forks, rake teeth, small wheels, golf-club heads, chisel handles, and jeweler blocks. Indians and early settlers used dried Dogwood bark to treat fevers

328

and during the Civil War as a quinine substitute. Frayed Dogwood twigs were sometimes used as toothbrushes as the sap was supposed to inhibit dental problems. The Indians also obtained a red dye from the roots and spear shafts from the stems.

Pioneers knew they had good agricultural soil if Dogwood were found on it naturally. Not only does Flowering Dogwood prefer a rich soil, but it helps build its own. The scarlet leaves that fall in autumn break down rapidly, releasing several valuable minerals including calcium which moderates the soil (pH) for better growth. Many species of birds feed on the bright red fruits and Flowering Dogwood is considered one of the very best choices as a landscape ornamental to attract wildlife. The state champion Flowering Dogwood is 37 feet tall and has a 49-inch trunk circumference and a crown spread of 46 feet. It is located at the Longhorn Army Ammunition Depot near Marshall, in Harrison County.

ROUGH-LEAF DOGWOOD. *Cornus drummondii.*

Usually a thicket-forming shrub but it may become a small tree about 20 feet tall. It is most often found near creeks, in moist woods, or along the edge of woods in the central and eastern parts of the state. Rough-Leaf Dogwood is distinguished from Flowering Dogwood by having rough-hairy leaves, small white flowers borne in late spring or early summer without the large showy bracts, having white fruits instead of red, and generally forming thickets from root suckers.

329

FRINGE TREE

Chionanthus virginicus.
Grancy Gray Beard.
Ornamental small tree to about 20 feet tall with a slender trunk and an irregularly-rounded crown.

Leaves — Opposite, deciduous, somewhat leathery, dark green and smooth above, paler below, pubescent when young but becoming smooth with age, 4-8 inches long and about half as wide. The petiole is often dark colored near the base. The leaves turn a bright yellow in the fall.

Flowers — In mid spring with the young leaves, the sexes appearing on separate trees as loose hanging clusters up to 6 inches long of white narrow four-lobed petals about 1 inch long. The sweet subtle fragrance is most pronounced from the female flowers.

330

Fruit — Ripening in late summer (only on the female trees) as dark blue, with a whitish bloom, drupe about ⅓ inch in diameter and up to 1 inch long, containing 1-3 oval-shaped seeds about ⅓ inch long.

Twigs — Moderately stout, stiff, green at first but turning tan or light brown later with prominent rounded lenticels, raised leaf scars, and scaly buds. The terminal bud somewhat round, chestnut brown, with definite overlapping scales. Some leaf scars may be sub-opposite to almost alternate.

Bark — Thin, tight, tan, smooth when young, eventually turning into small ridges and shallow furrows.

Fringe Tree is usually found in nature as an understory tree in moist woods and along stream banks throughout the Piney Woods of East Texas west to near Brazos County. It is very conspicuous when in bloom and easy to recognize from the roadway during this time. From a distance the flowers have an appearance vaguely resembling the whiskers of an old man, hence one of the common names "Grancy Gray Beard." The male plants have the showier flowers, and the fruits are relished by birds. Fringe Tree bark has many reputed medicinal qualities and is used as a decoction, tincture, or external poultice for wounds and skin irritations. Its main uses are as a laxative, diuretic, febrifuge, and tonic. Other uses include curing acute dyspepsia, liver ailments, and for overall beneficial effect on the kidneys. Unfortunately, as with many other species of small trees, Fringe Trees have a beautiful wood that never receives attention because they do not reach merchantable size. The wood is heavy, hard, and with a very attractive grain that takes a good polish.

SWAMP PRIVET. *Forestiera acuminata.*

A large shrub or small tree with several trunks to 8 inches in diameter and up to 30 feet tall. Male and female flowers are on separate plants, small, yellowish, without petals and are borne from the leaf axils. Female flowers are followed by football-shaped, blue to black, thin fleshed fruits about 1 inch long and containing a single hard spindle-shaped seed. The yellowish-green opposite leaves are about 2 to 4 inches long and 1 inch or more in width. It is basically a swamp-loving tree restricted to floodplains, creek and river bottoms scattered about the eastern third of the state, venturing westward to the Victoria County area.

WHITE ASH

Fraxinus americana.
Medium sized tree about 70 feet tall with a trunk diameter of 2-3 feet. Trees in forest conditions have a narrow crown and long, straight unbranched trunk. In the open, the trees tend to form a low-branched round top and a relatively short trunk.

Leaves — Opposite, compound, deciduous, about 1 foot long. Leaflets 7, sometimes 9; 3-5 inches long and 1½ to 3 inches wide. Deep green above and pale to whitish underneath. Leaves turning yellow to purple in the fall.

Flowers — In early spring, from last year's shoots, before or with the expanding new leaves. Male flowers appearing as clusters of stamens but each individual flower consisting of 2-3 stamens and a minute slightly four-lobed calyx. The female flowers in loose clusters of many flowers each with no corolla but a single pistil and a deeply four-lobed calyx.

333

Fruit — Ripening August and September in dense clusters of cigar-shaped seeds attached at the base to a narrow oar-shaped wing that is about 3/16 of an inch wide. (Green Ash, described later, has fruits which are narrower—1/3 inch wide—and the seed is almost half enclosed by the wing rather than attached at the base.)

Twigs — Slender, rigid, and round in cross section, sometimes swollen at the nodes. The dark brown or black buds have a suede appearance and are nestled in the notch-shaped leaf scars. (Green Ash buds rest entirely on top of flat-topped, half-round leaf scars.)

Bark — Smooth and light brown when young, soon developing a very distinctive pattern most often likened to a basket weave of interlacing diamond shapes. The ridges are light gray to somewhat silvery and the background furrows almost black on older trees.

White Ash is a fairly common tree throughout East Texas westward to the Trinity River Valley. It is most often found in fairly moist (but also in well-drained) woods, upper bottomland situations, and coves. Richer soils are preferred and young trees are considered somewhat sun-loving, becoming increasingly intolerant of shade and competition from other species with age. Young trees will often persist in the lower forest until an opening presents itself. The trees then grow rapidly, taking advantage of the space.

White Ash wood is whitish with a light brownish heartwood and distinct growth rings. It is heavy and hard with a nice straight grain which makes it easy to split as firewood logs, and the wood is highly valued for its strength and elasticity. These qualities make it superb for tool handles and athletic equipment such as baseball bats and long oars. Indians used the straight branchlets for arrows and the wood was also good for bows. Ash as a cabinet wood and veneer has come into its own. Synthetics, alloys, and lamination have largely replaced ash in its former uses but the wood is still used routinely for pallet boxes and planing-mill products like trim.

As a landscape tree, White Ash does best on or near its natural range and preferred site conditions. Off-site trees tend to get borers easily and weaken. White Ash should be given plenty of room to develop the rounded crown. Female trees reseed themselves prolifically but there are several seedless male selections that also give good fall colors of rich purple to bronzy red. White Ash in general has a good growth rate, is relatively free from pests and disease problems, and gives a good medium shade. Many species of birds and mammals feed on the seeds which are produced in abundance.

TEXAS ASH. *Fraxinus texensis.*

A small tree to about 30 feet tall that differs from other native ash species by only having 5 (rarely 7) roundish leaflets and being normally restricted to limestone hills and bluffs throughout the Edwards Plateau to the Colorado River area and north to the Collin County area. This tree was once considered a variety of White Ash and can barely be separated from it in areas where the ranges overlap. Texas Ash makes a nice landscape tree in areas within its range that are not thin soiled and exposed.

335

BERLANDIER ASH

Fraxinus berlandieriana.
Fresno, Mexican Ash.
A small to medium sized tree to about 40 feet tall with a broad, rounded crown and a trunk to several feet in diameter, often branching early when grown in the open. Forest-grown specimens may have long slender trunks that branch much higher.

Leaves — Opposite, compound, deciduous, up to 10 inches long with 3-5 leaflets that are about 3-4 inches long and ½ to 1½ inches wide. Dark green, smooth and shiny above, somewhat paler and occasionally slightly hairy beneath (along the mid vein and major vein axils).

Flowers — In spring, before or with the expanding new leaves, the sexes borne on separate trees. The male flowers are without petals and in relatively tight clusters; the female flowers are in elongate looser clusters and have no petals but a single pistil.

Fruit — Ripening in the fall, 1 inch or more in length and about ¼ inch wide. The cylindrical seed is tapered at both ends and at least ⅓ enclosed by the wing.

Twigs — Slender, stout, round in cross section but somewhat flattened and / or swollen at the nodes. Light green at first but becoming light brown later. The dark brown buds have a suede appearance.

Bark — Gray to light brown at first but becoming much darker with age and soon developing the "ash bark" pattern of interwoven diamonds of flat-topped ridges and shallow fissures.

Berlandier Ash is normally found along creeks and rivers from the southern Edwards Plateau and south into Mexico. The wood is somewhat inferior to other ash species but it is good for fuel. This tree has been widely planted throughout South and Coastal Texas where it is often marketed under the name "Arizona Ash" which is now considered a different species (see below). Its hardy nature, ease of reproduction, fast growth, and good shade have caused Mexican Ash to be terribly overplanted, often on poor sites. It is now deemed a "weed tree" by organizations like the Texas Forest and Agricultural Extension Services because of its relatively short life span, susceptibility to pests and diseases under some conditions, and habit of dropping small dead branches constantly. At least one seedless variety, Fantex Ash, has been developed and does well under most conditions.

Ash bark and leaves contain a glucoside called fraxin that has been used as a tonic and febrifuge. The leaves have been used in a decoction to treat yellow fever, malaria, gout, rheumatism, and for its purgative properties. The national champion Berlandier Ash, presently in a state of decline, is 44 feet tall with a crown spread of 40 feet and a trunk circumference of 194 inches. It is located in the Santa Ana National Wildlife Refuge in Hidalgo County.

VELVET ASH. *Fraxinus velutina.*
Arizona Ash, Fresno.

Medium sized tree 40 feet tall with a broad rounded crown. In Texas it is restricted to canyons and arroyos in the Trans-Pecos mountains. It has been widely planted as an ornamental (many trees sold as Arizona Ash are actually Berlandier Ash), shade, or street tree. It differs from Berlandier by having uniformly hairy leaf undersides, the wing of the fruit extending to above the middle of the seed body, and its natural range being the Trans-Pecos mountains, whereas Berlandier Ash grows in South and South Central Texas.

FRAGRANT ASH. *Fraxinus cuspidata.*
Flowering Ash.

A small tree to about 20 feet tall from the mountains of the Trans-Pecos area of Texas. It is unique among our native ashes by having flowers with petals somewhat resembling the Fringe Tree of the eastern part of the state. This is a handsome tree when in bloom and deserves more attention as an ornamental but its cultural requirements are not yet fully understood.

338

GREGG ASH. *Fraxinus greggii.*
Escobilla.

A shrub or small tree barely 15 feet tall found on rocky slopes, limestone canyons, and along streams of Southwest Texas in the area of Brewster, Terrell, and Val Verde counties. It can readily be separated from other native ash species by the comparatively small, usually evergreen, leaves about 1 inch long with typically 3 but up to 7 narrow leaflets ¼ inch or less wide. It is presently being tried as a commercial ornamental outside its natural range. Where it grows naturally the tree is a good deer browse and in Mexico the stiff branches are sometimes used for brooms.

GREEN ASH

Fraxinus pennsylvanica.
Medium sized tree 50 feet or more in height, with a somewhat narrowed crown and a trunk that may be swollen at the base when growing in old sloughs.

Leaves — Opposite, compound, deciduous, about 10 to 12 inches in length and consisting of 7-9 leaflets that are about 5 inches long and one inch wide, bright green above and only slightly paler below, turning yellow or sometimes shades of purple in autumn.

Flowers — In early spring before or with the expanding new leaves, the male and female flowers borne on separate trees. Male flowers in relatively tight clusters that appear as masses of stamens because each individual flower has no petals, usually 2 stamens and a tiny four-lobed calyx. Female flowers are in more open elongated clusters with a single pistil and a more deeply-lobed calyx.

Fruit — Becoming ripe in early fall, 1-2 inches long, the wing about ⅛ inch wide and enclosing at least ½ of the narrowly cylindrical and long tapering seed. (White Ash seeds are attached at the base and not much enclosed by the wing.)

Twigs — Slender, round in cross section between nodes, hairy but sometimes smooth the first year, green at first and later turning tan to light brown. Leaf buds dark red-brown, sitting on top of a half-round leaf scar. (Most other native ash species have buds that sit, to some degree, down into a notch in the leaf scar.)

Bark — Light brown when young, turning gray brown to black and developing the typical ash bark—the basket weave effect of interwoven diamond patterns of narrow flat-topped ridges—at an early age.

Green Ash is the most widespread ash species in North America. It is found in East, Central, and Coastal Texas west to about the Guadalupe River Valley. It is almost always associated with water and areas that are periodically flooded such as sloughs, creeks, and river bottoms. In these areas they frequently replace cottonwood and willow as the dominant tree after a disturbance but are considered somewhat shade intolerant. Along with Sugarberry and American Elm, Green Ash forms an association of species that often dominates creek and river bottoms throughout the eastern United States.

Green Ash wood is heavier and somewhat more brittle than White Ash but is generally used for the same purposes. Even though Green Ash is naturally associated with waterways, it will grow on a variety of sites. It is fast growing, relatively pest and disease free, gives good shade, but does poorly on dry exposed sites with thin soils. Some seedless male varieties have been developed, with Marshall's Seedless being one of the best. In some areas it was formerly a popular shelterbelt tree. Green Ash reliably produces a heavy seed crop. The seeds and leaves are eaten by a number of wildlife species. The state champion Green Ash is 78 feet tall with a crown spread of 68 feet and a trunk circumference of 145 inches. It is located on U.S. Army Corps of Engineers land near Grapevine Lake in Tarrant County. Green Ash is the state tree of North Dakota.

CAROLINA ASH. *Fraxinus caroliniana.*

A swamp understory tree that rarely gets more than 30 feet tall. It is found deep in East Texas, west to about the Neches River Valley. The features that distinguish this ash from other native species are that it is a true swamp or old slough tree, has 5-7 leaflets, and the fruit is very distinctive with the seed totally enclosed by a broad wing up to 1 inch wide.

CHASTE TREE

Vitex agnus-castus.
Sage Tree.

Strongly scented shrub or small tree 20 feet tall with a low, wide-spreading crown, often with many crooked or leaning trunks.

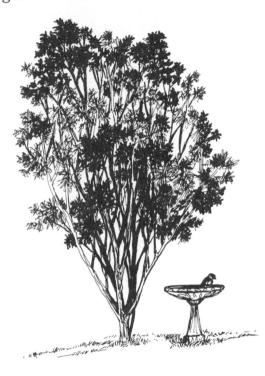

Leaves — Opposite, deciduous, palmately compound usually with 5-7 leaflets, the middle one longer at 3-4 inches in length. Dark green or gray green above and densely white hairy beneath. The tree is easily recognized by the strong scent the leaves emit when crushed.

Flowers — Mainly in late spring but may continue sporadically up to fall in branched, dense, terminal spikes up to 7 inches long. The perfect five-lobed flowers are about ⅓

343

inch long with 4 exerted stamens. Blue and purple are the most common colors but pink and white varieties are also cultivated.

Fruit—Maturing in the fall as upright, terminal, round, woody drupes slightly more than an ⅛ inch wide with a four-celled stone. Also strongly scented like the leaves.

Twigs—Thin, often showing winter tip dieback, powdery gray or gray, with small powdery gray buds. The winter appearance of the tree is overall very twiggy.

Bark—Thin, smooth, and gray when young but quickly breaking into broad ridges and shallow fissures with a gray stringy nature.

Chaste Tree is a native of southern Europe and western Asia but has become naturalized in Northeast and Central Texas, where it is most often associated with creeks or streams. There is a good population along IH 35 south of Austin. The plant is showy when in bloom and is an old garden favorite. An oil is expressed from the seeds which are also credited with having sedative properties. A tea made from the leaves is said to be an anti-aphrodisiac and was reportedly used by monks to help them remain chaste. The leaves can be used to spice foods and a perfume can be made from the flowers.

344

NORTHERN CATALPA

Catalpa speciosa.
Indian Bean, Cigar Tree.
A medium sized tree to about 50 feet tall with a low, broadly-rounded crown from a relatively short trunk two feet or more in diameter.

Leaves — Whorled or opposite, deciduous, 6 to 10 inches in length, 4 to 8 inches wide. Soft hairy on the underside and towards the petiole on the upperside.

Flowers — Late spring to early summer, in showy terminal panicles up to 8 inches long held above the foliage. The fragrant trumpet-shaped flowers, about 1½ inches long, are mostly white, the inner surface marked with yellow stripes and brown-purple spots. The stripes in the flower throat are "bee guides", serving to direct these insects to the nectar source.

345

Fruit — Ripening in the fall, a narrow cylindrical beanlike capsule up to 16 inches in length and ½ inch in diameter, splitting down the middle revealing many one-inch-long, thin, papery flakes containing two egg-yolklike seeds with a silver fringe at each end.

Twigs — Stout with a large pith, greenish at first, turning gray to brown later, covered with many whitish lenticels. Easily distinguished by the large whorled or opposite leaf scars and small, scaly, rounded buds.

Bark — Relatively thin, gray turning brown with long narrow scales peeling from the edges.

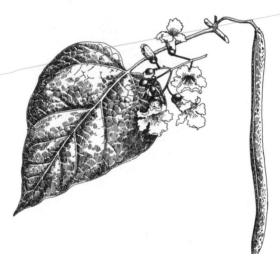

In the wild, Northern Catalpa is most often found along creeks and streams in East Texas. Recent research indicates this tree may have originally been confined to Jasper and Hardin counties but it has been widely cultivated as an ornamental and planted throughout the state. Catalpa wood is moderately soft with a straight grain. The thick heartwood is grayish brown—sometimes lavender-tinged surrounded by a thin pale gray sapwood. It is very durable when in contact with the soil and was once favored for fence posts and railroad ties. The attractive color and grain give it good cabinetmaking possibilities. When in full bloom, the Catalpa is one of the most beautiful large sized native trees and is commonly grown for its floral display and large attractive heart-shaped leaves. Its quick growth, disease and pest resistance, and ability to grow almost anywhere except on thin, dry, alkaline soils make Catalpa a desirable ornamental. One unique quality of Catalpa is that it hosts the Catalpa worm, a two-inch-long black-and-white-striped caterpillar which is great fishing bait.

The pods and seeds are said to have sedative and antispasmodic qualities but in large doses cause weakness and vomiting. Catalpa bark has been used to treat intestinal parasites, and the flowers, when handled, can cause dermatitis in some people. Catalpa pods, split in two, can be soaked in water and used to weave small baskets. Youngsters used to try to smoke the fruit pods, giving rise to the name Cigar Tree. This is one of the few Texas trees that has retained its native American name. Creek Indians called it *kuthlpa* which means "head with wings," presumably referring to the winged seeds.

SOUTHERN CATALPA. *Catalpa bignoniodes.*

Southern Catalpa differs from the above species by being taller, having more flowers per cluster, and the leaves short pointed instead of long pointed at the tip. It is widely cultivated as an ornamental across the eastern two-thirds of Texas.

DESERT WILLOW

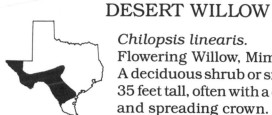

Chilopsis linearis.
Flowering Willow, Mimbre.
A deciduous shrub or small tree up to
35 feet tall, often with a crooked trunk
and spreading crown.

Leaves — Willow-like, opposite or alternate, narrow pointed, ranging from 3 to 10 inches long, pale green, often sticky.

Flowers — Showy, tubular, orchid-like, usually lavender, but white and burgundy forms exist. Blooms June to October.

Fruit — Narrow pod, light brown, 5 to 8 inches long, containing flat, hairy-tufted, winged seeds within.

Twigs — Green to light brown at first, becoming darker later.

Bark — Smooth when young, dark brown, ridged and scaly when older.

348

The Desert Willow is found along streams, dry washes, and arroyos throughout the Trans-Pecos of Texas up to North Texas near Wichita Falls and southeast to the Corpus Christi area. It has naturalized in the Llano Uplift area. It also ranges west into California and south to Mexico. Desert Willow is a popular ornamental planted throughout the central and southern portions of the state. This plant, so named because of its long narrow leaves, is not even closely related to the willow; it is of the same family as Catalpa, with the characteristic tubular flowers and long narrow fruits.

The Desert Willow is very adaptable and will grow under a variety of soil and moisture conditions. Commonly found along washes, it plays an important role in erosion control and is widely planted for that purpose. The wood is light and brittle but durable and was a favorite among some western Indians for making bows. It is also used for fence building and fuel. In Mexico, the tree is called *Mimbre* and the young branches are used for weaving baskets; dried Mimbre flowers are sold in Mexican markets as a remedy for coughs. Bees are quite fond of this plant and are attracted to the purple stripes of the flower tube. Bees have excellent ultra-violet vision and these flower stripes or "bee guides," as some call them, are quite pronounced in the ultra-violet spectrum and aid in directing the bees to the nectar. Hummingbirds are also frequent visitors to the flowers of this tree.

The Desert Willow is an attractive plant easily grown from seed or cuttings. Although it forms a nice small tree, some prefer to keep it cut back to a shrub form because it blooms off new wood and this encourages flowering.

ELDERBERRY

Sambucus canadensis.
American Elder.
A large shrub or small tree to about 20 feet tall with several stems and often spreading by underground suckers.

Leaves — Opposite, deciduous, compound to about one foot long with 5 to 11 toothed leaflets 2-5 inches long and about half as wide. The leaflets are green on top and paler below.

Flowers — Appearing in late spring through early summer, somewhat flattened as small white 5-petaled perfect flowers ⅛ inch wide in large clusters up to 1 foot across.

Fruit — Ripening from mid to late summer, often maturing while still in the act of flowering. The juicy berry-like drupe is black-purple and almost ¼ inch long when ripe; it holds 3-4 small yellow seeds. These fruits are edible when ripe but have a somewhat bitter aftertaste.

Twigs — Greenish to maroon, turning brown later, often with warty bumps, a large pith, and small parts of last year's inflorescence terminally attached.

Bark — Smooth and gray brown with whitish lenticels at first, becoming darker and roughened or furrowed when mature.

Elderberry is usually found near creeks and streams, where it commonly forms small thickets throughout the eastern half of the state. This plant is most famous for its edible ripe berries that have been used for a variety of culinary and medicinal purposes. They are best noted for the outstanding wines (made famous by the play *Arsenic and Old Lace*) and jellies they make but are also high in vitamin C content and can be used to make a refreshing non-alcoholic drink. The flower clusters can be dipped in batter and fried into fritters. Although the ripe berries and flower clusters are edible, the unripe berries, roots, stems, and leaves are considered poisonous, causing vomiting and diarrhea. Virtually every part of the Elderberry has been used for medicinal purposes and could almost be called "good for what ails you." Juice made from ripe berries was used for cough syrups, gargles, and other cold treatments. The flowers were made into a tea to treat fevers, colds, rheumatism, and as a wash for sore eyes. External applications of the leaves, roots, and bark formed a poultice to treat swellings, tumors, sore joints, and broken bones. These parts are also supposed to have cosmetic properties such as removing spots, freckles, and preserving and softening the skin.

Elderberry is an important wildlife food. The foliage is sometimes browsed, but the real value lies in the berries which are consumed by many species of animals. Songbirds are so eager they often eat the fruit while still green.

MEXICAN ELDER. *Sambucus mexicana.*

A shrub or small tree almost 30 feet tall found in the lower elevations of the West Texas mountains. It differs from American Elder by having a more western distribution and usually 3 to 5 leaflets. Medicinally, it was used by the Indians and in Mexico for the same purposes as the eastern species.

RUSTY BLACKHAW

Viburnum rufidulum.
Small distinctive tree to 25 feet or a large shrub with a spreading, rounded crown and rumored to occasionally form thickets by root suckers.

Leaves — Opposite, deciduous, about 3 inches long, glossy, dark green above and rusty hairy on the veins below, turning pink to dark purple before dropping in the fall.

Flowers — Borne in mid spring after the leaves unfold as small, white, five-lobed fragrant flowers in dense flattened, but slightly rounded, clusters. Each individual flower is about ¼ inch wide and contains 5 stamens and a single pistil.

Fruit — Ripening in the fall as loose clusters of dark blue football-shaped edible fleshy fruits, about ½ inch long with a single somewhat flattened stonelike seed.

Twigs — Stiff and somewhat stout, gray to reddish brown with a distinctive, pointed, terminal bud about ⅓-inch long made of two opposing scales covered with dense rusty brown hairs. The lateral buds hug the stem and are also covered with rusty brown hairs.

Bark — Smooth and gray at first, becoming almost black, with a distinctive blocky or checkered appearance with age.

Rusty Blackhaw is usually an understory tree associated with streams, fence lines, or moist woods found predominantly in East and Central Texas with a small population out in the Davis Mountains. It is a handsome plant with its shiny foliage, abundant flowers, pretty fall color, and curious bark. It is not particular as to soils, will tolerate some shade, and is fairly drought tolerant. The edible

fruits have a raisin-like taste and can be eaten either raw or cooked. Pioneers used them in jellies, sauces, and stews. Wildlife also enjoy the fruits. The hard yellow wood has a mildly unpleasant odor when sawn. This tree has good ornamental potential with its rugged nature and attractive appearance.

BLACKHAW. *Viburnum prunifolium.*

Blackhaw is somewhat uncommon in the forests of East Texas and is very similar to Rusty Blackhaw differing only by lacking the rust-colored hairs on the lower leaf surfaces. The root bark of these two species was used in the treatment of dysmenorrhea and as a tonic and had an official listing in the U.S. Pharmacopoeia.

Selected References
and
Glossary

SELECTED REFERENCES

Bailey, L.H. *The Standard Cyclopedia of Horticulture.* New York: The Macmillan Company, 1935.

Correll, Donavan S., and Marshall C. Johnston. *Manual of the Vascular Plants of Texas.* Texas: Texas Research Foundation, 1970.

Elias, Thomas S. *The Complete Trees of North America, Field Guide and Natural History.* New York: Book Division, Times Mirror Magazines, Inc., 1980.

Jones, Fred B. *Flora of the Texas Coastal Bend.* Texas: Mission Press, 1982.

Lynch, Brother Daniel, C.S.C. *Native and Naturalized Woody Plants of Austin & the Hill Country.* Saint Edward's University, 1981.

Peattie, Donald Culross. *A Natural History of Trees of Eastern and Central America.* Massachusetts: The Riverside Press, Cambridge, 1950.

———. *A Natural History of Western Trees.* Massachusetts: The Riverside Press, Cambridge, 1953.

Standley, Paul C. *Trees and Shrubs of Mexico.* Washington D.C.: Government Printing Office, 1920–1926.

Texas Forest Service. *Famous Trees of Texas.* Texas: Texas A&M University Press, 1984.

Turner, B.L. *The Legumes of Texas.* Texas: University of Texas Press, 1959.

356

Vines, Robert A. *Trees, Shrubs and Woody Vines of the Southwest.* Texas: University of Texas Press, 1960.

Warnock, Barton H. *Wildflowers of the Big Bend Country, Texas.* Texas: Sul Ross State University, 1970.

————. *Wildflowers of the Davis Mountains and the Marathon Basin, Texas.* Texas: Sul Ross State University, 1977.

————. *Wildflowers of the Guadalupe Mountains and the Sand Dune Country, Texas.* Texas: Sul Ross State University, 1974.

GLOSSARY

Arborescent - Having a single trunk or tending to be more up-right as opposed to a multi-trunk shrub or climbing vine.

Axils - The area between the top of the leaf base and the branch. Many flowers are borne from the axillary region.

Carpels - The lobes of the flower's ovary.

Climax cover - When the shade tolerant species dominate and perpetuate themselves in the forest canopy they create the final stage of plant succession known as the climax community. The Oak-Hickory forest type is probably one of the more widespread climax communities in Texas.

Cultivar - A distinctive form or individual characteristic that has been perpetuated either by seed or vegetatively through cuttings, graftings, buddings, etc.

"Den trees" - Large, often hollow, trees which provide home or shelter to many of the forest wildlife species.

Terminal winter dieback - The end portion of the branch or twig which has been killed by winter freezes.

Disjunct - Isolated populations or groups of individuals which occur outside the normal range of the species.

Distinct - Having a certain unique characteristic.

Drupe - A fleshy fruit containing a single seed.

Escaped cultivation - Plants, usually exotic specimens, that have been cultivated outside their normal range and have successfully reseeded themselves to the point of becoming an established member of the local flora.

358

Exerted stamens - Male flower organs which usually grow on long filaments projecting beyond the immediate flower area.

Febrifuge - A chemical or potion used to lower the temperature of a fever.

Fusiform gall rust - A fungal disease that alternates primarily between certain oak species and the southern pines. The harmful effects are most drastic on the pine species where the rust can infect and completely encircle a stem and kill it. Oaks merely bear disfigured foliage as a result of the fungal infection.

Glabrous - Smooth, without hairs or other distinguishing features such as glands, scales, teeth, etc.

Glaucescent - Having a slightly whitish bloom or pale waxy covering.

Glaucous - Having a distinctive whitish slightly waxy covering.

Habitat - As the plant occurs in nature or in its natural surroundings.

Inflorescence - The flowers and their supporting stalks viewed as a whole.

Intergrade - When two species/varieties ranges meet and some hybridization occurs which blurs the distinctive features of both the parents.

Lanceolate - Having the general shape of a spear blade.

Lenticels - Breathing pores in the bark usually represented by dots, bumps, or horizontal lens-shaped markings.

Mott - An isolated small clump of trees, often of the same species, usually occurring in the middle of a grassland.

Mycorrhizal - A beneficial relationship between a green plant and a fungus species living in or near the plant's roots. Both entities derive nutrients from the other's involvement by the exchange of chemicals.

Obovate - Egg-shaped, being widest toward the leaf tip.

Palmately compound - A compound leaf with the leaflets radiating from a center point, somewhat resembling the fingers in a hand.

Panicle - Flower clusters that are branched more than once resulting in a relatively spreading inflorescence.

Petiole - The stalk that supports a leaf, the structure between the branch and the leaf blade.

Petiolate - Having a petiole, a leaf with a petiole.

Pinnae - The individual leaflets of a compound leaf.

Pinnately lobed - A simple leaf with lobes that originate perpendicular to the main vein and somewhat resemble a pinnate compound leaf.

Pioneer type - A plant community of species that is the first to colonize disturbed areas.

Pistil - The female portion of the flower.

Populations - Groups of a particular plant species found at a given location.

Pubescent - Covered with short soft hairs.

Racemes - Elongated, relatively tight flower clusters consisting of many short-stalked flowers along an unbranched central axis.

Rachis - The central stem of a pinnately compound leaf.

Resaca - A natural or man-made slough or ox-bow lake situation, usually the former course of a river.

Index

INDEX

364